Independence and a New Partnership

IN CATHOLIC HIGHER EDUCATION

Independence and a New Partnership

IN CATHOLIC HIGHER EDUCATION

Alice Gallin, O.S.U.

UNIVERSITY OF NOTRE DAME PRESS

Notre Dame, Indiana

Manufactured in the United States of America

Book design by Wendy McMillen
Set in 12/14 Adobe Caslon by Books International
Printed and bound by Thomson-Shore, Inc.

Library of Congress Cataloging-in-Publication Data

Gallin, Alice.
 Independence and a new partnership in Catholic higher education /
Alice Gallin.
  p. cm.
 Includes bibliographical references and index.
 ISBN 0-268-01478-7 (alk. paper)
  1. Catholic universities and colleges—United States—
History—20th century. I. Title.
 LC501.G35 1996
 377'.8273—dc20   95-47144
                                                        CIP

∞ The paper used in this publication meets the minimum requirements of the
American National Standard for Information Sciences—Permanence of
Paper for Printed Library Materials.

To all the men and women who hold Catholic colleges and universities "in trust," in gratitude for the partnership developed over the past thirty years.

Contents

Acknowledgments

In the fall of 1992 a small group of willing helpers met with me at the University of Notre Dame to recall the events surrounding the move to independent governing boards. Rev. Theodore M. Hesburgh, C.S.C., was the gracious host and was joined by his friend and colleague for many years, Mr. Edmund Stephan, who was the first lay chair of the board at Notre Dame as well as the architect of its bylaws. From Saint Louis University came Rev. Paul Reinert, S.J., and his first lay chair, Mr. Daniel Schlafly. A third important president, Ann Ida Gannon, B.V.M., brought to us the distinctive story of a women's college which forged ahead to implement the decrees of Vatican II. For years, Sister Ann Ida was the model and mentor for many other women presidents. To assist me with their insights and questions, two of my colleagues in the field of history, Dr. Philip Gleason of the University of Notre Dame and Dr. David O'Brien of the College of the Holy Cross, agreed to be members of the group. The important supporter of the project, The Lilly Endowment, was well represented by Jeanne Knoerle, S.P.

For two and a half days this group reflected on their roles and stimulated me to pursue the intriguing topic of the transition to independent boards by Catholic colleges and universities. Their encouragement and support never flagged, and they have continued to offer help at every step of the way.

Their oral history led me next to the archives of the universities to seek the relevant documents. I received the most courteous and helpful assistance from the archivists at Notre

Dame, Saint Louis, Mundelein, Loyola of Chicago, the College of New Rochelle, Fordham University, College of the Holy Cross, Trinity College in Washington, D.C., Saint Michael's College in Vermont, St. Bonaventure University, and The Catholic University of America. I am also grateful to the administration of CUA for my appointment as Visiting Research Scholar in 1992 and subsequent years. The library and files of the Association of Catholic Colleges and Universities, the Association of Governing Boards, the American Association of Colleges and Universities, and the American Association of University Professors were also placed at my disposal.

In dealing with the legal issues, canonical and civil, I needed a great deal of wise and knowledgeable counsel, and I received it in the reading and rereading of my manuscript by Rev. Frederick R. McManus and Rev. Robert Kennedy of the Canon Law Department at The Catholic University of America and in several conversations with Mr. Charles Wilson. Critical attention to early drafts was also contributed by Rev. John F. Murphy, former executive director of ACCU, Dr. Mary Russo, O.S.U., archivist at the College of New Rochelle, and Dr. Philip Gleason of Notre Dame.

The finished product owes much to my editor at the University of Notre Dame Press, Ms. Rebecca DeBoer; without her it would have been far less readable.

Especially do I wish to express my gratitude to my Ursuline community for their willingness to support me in this endeavor and for their never-failing interest in its progress. My friends and relatives have also kept me focused on the task without ever letting me feel isolated because of the need for solitude when working. The funding provided by the Lilly Endowment was crucial and for that I am indeed grateful.

Preface

The late 1960s witnessed changes in American Catholic higher education that would radically alter the 300 colleges and universities that constituted this cohort.[1] For the next three decades they would struggle with the ambiguity that was thus introduced into their identity as "Catholic." Indeed current discussions about the "secularization" of American Catholic colleges and universities often point to the late 1960s as the time when they began their path down the slippery slope to "secularization."[2] In this context "secularization" has a negative connotation, implying that the values of the world, a world seen as devoid of religious meaning, have triumphed over the forces of faith and religion. In conversations about the ways in which Catholic colleges and universities are or are not still "Catholic," a link is often made between the process of secularization and the moment when religious communities, under the leadership of their college presidents, "gave away" their colleges to lay persons.

In the hope of setting the record straight, I have undertaken this study of the transfer of governance from communities to boards of trustees with predominantly lay membership. Until the 1960s, most Catholic colleges and universities were governed by trustees who, in fact, were the members of religious community governing councils and their major superiors; if they had lay trustees, these were regarded as merely advisory. The transfer of real power from the organs of religious authority to legal boards composed of elected lay and religious members is what I denote as "laicization"; it did not intend or imply "secularization."

At the time of this transfer what was the makeup of the cohort of Catholic colleges and universities? Several attempts were made in the 1960s to gather data describing the institutions. The studies which were published as a result of such data collection are not consistent regarding the number of colleges and universities, the size and composition of their student bodies, and the makeup of their boards of trustees. Perhaps the most significant and reliable survey is that done by Charles Ford and Edgar Roy at the request of the National Catholic Educational Association, College and University Department in 1964–65. This study separates information about diocesan seminaries, colleges for religious sisters (Sister Formation Colleges), and institutions for communities of religious men, giving data for faculty, accreditation, and funding as well as more general items. In my work I am dealing only with the colleges and universities designed for lay men and women.

Philip Gleason, in his excellent history of Catholic higher education in the twentieth century, concludes by saying that the 1960s "mark the end of an era in the history of Catholic higher education."[3] Gleason's theme throughout his work is the confrontation of Catholic universities with modernity and their ultimate adaptation to it, a metaphor of the process of inculturation. Certainly, the shift in governance was a significant part of that adaptation.

Gleason has maintained elsewhere that until the late 1960s there was no serious discussion of "Catholic identity." He points out that it was clear to both internal and external constituencies that the colleges founded by religious communities and/or dioceses were "Catholic."[4] However, the increased participation of lay persons in administration and governance created a new dynamic in the relationship between college and religious community; it also changed the college relationship with the Catholic community and with ecclesiastical authority. Without control by religious communities, what would keep the colleges Catholic?

In order to trace this process of laicization of governance with the specificity that is needed to make judgments about the motives of those who initiated it and the effects that it had on subsequent history, I have selected seven institutions as case studies: the College of New Rochelle, Saint Louis University, the University of Notre Dame, Mundelein College, University of Portland, Saint Michael's College, and Fordham University. These institutions differed from one another in size, history, founding religious communities, student bodies, faculty, and governing structures in the mid-1960s. Some are women's colleges, some men's or coed; they are located in different states, although two of them are in New York, thus having a common task of seeking to meet the criteria of eligibility for Bundy money but taking two different routes to that end. All seven differed significantly from one another in terms of endowment and fund-raising capacity. On the other hand, a network of Catholic college presidents, legal counsels, and consultants existed that gave a certain unity to the movement toward independent boards.

The method I have used in studying these institutions combines study of the archival materials of the period and personal interviews with some of the main players in the events. The minutes of the boards of trustees, both before and after the date of transfer of authority, and the speeches, written memoranda, and other vehicles by which the goals were explained and argued were particularly helpful as a check on individual memories, while the personal recollections often aided interpretation. In reconstructing the historical events it was important to know how the case was argued at the time, not only how it was remembered when its effects were perceived. The variety among the institutions studied allows us, I think, to come to some general conclusions about the actions and the motives behind them at this special moment in Catholic higher education.

I have dealt with the individual stories in chapter 2 and have done so chronologically according to the date the decision to transfer governing power was made by the appropriate authority. In some cases, detailed arrangements between the religious community and the college/university took one or two more years, so the dating is somewhat arbitrary. In each case I shall attempt to place the events in the context of the college or university's earlier history, to describe the reasons given for making the changes, and to identify and evaluate the significant leaders and their work.

Since all these leaders utilized the legal opinion of Msgr. John McGrath, a canon lawyer at The Catholic University of America,[5] and since they all were working within the limits of American civil and constitutional law, I have dealt with their legal concerns in a separate chapter. In that area there remain many unresolved questions.

From this study of the transformation of boards of trustees in Catholic colleges and universities several conclusions will emerge:

1. The addition of lay men and women to the governing boards was a necessary step in the growth and development of Catholic higher education. The reasons for taking this step were varied and complex.

2. There was no one model for the new boards nor any single process by which they were created.

3. The inclusion of more lay persons in the governing authority of the institution was understood by lead-

ers of religious communities and those in the office of president as an effective response to the new theological teachings of Vatican Council II on the role of the laity in the church.

4. The decisions were based on an assumption that Msgr. McGrath's explanation of property ownership and control was a valid one.

Independence and a New Partnership

IN CATHOLIC HIGHER EDUCATION

ONE

Separation

"I knew that if I were going to see Notre Dame grow into a first-rate Catholic University I could no longer have to get permission from a Provincial every time I needed a new lawn mower!" Thus Rev. Theodore M. Hesburgh, C.S.C., described the fundamental reason for moving toward a new board of trustees for the university in 1967, a board that would be composed of lay and religious members and have true governing authority.[1]

Father Hesburgh's frustration with the intrusion of religious authority into the day-by-day affairs of the university was echoed by many of his presidential colleagues. In the 1964–65 Ford-Roy survey of Catholic colleges mentioned in the preface,[2] it was found that among the key issues identified by respondents, the role of religious orders in the colleges ranked second. It was preceded only by financial concerns, a topic which itself had an indirect relationship to the dependence of the college on the resources of the founding religious community and on the commingling of the income and expenses of several different institutions sponsored by that community.

While such financial interdependence of the Catholic college or university and the founding religious community was an important bond between the two, it also meant that the governance of the college relied on the organizational strength of the community and the wisdom of its leaders. In addition, the survey respondents pointed out, the strong sense of the particular sponsoring religious body's identity made inter-institutional cooperation among the colleges and universities very difficult. They were concerned that the history of competition among the orders and their institutions impeded the colleges' efforts toward cooperative long-range planning and possible consideration of mergers or other forms of significant affiliation between colleges. From this point of view, the multiplicity of Catholic colleges, intimately linked with different religious communities, was seen as fostering a highly competitive environment which was an obstacle to the attainment of an improved reputation among other institutions of higher education. Both academic excellence and financial viability depended on some mitigation of the competitive spirit and individualistic decision-making which had traditionally characterized the work of religious orders. It was time, the study suggested, to move away from colleges centered on the life of the religious community and into a new mode of "shared responsibility" with persons and agencies outside of the community.[3]

Father Paul Reinert, S.J., commenting on the Ford-Roy study (not yet published but circulating for critique), had this to say at the National Catholic Educational Association March 1967 meeting: "While there have been compensating advantages to the willingness of the various religious orders to shoulder the responsibility for most of our Catholic colleges and universities, and while the history of achievement in Catholic higher education has been written in large measure by religious men and women, I am convinced that the future depends on increased participation by laymen in both the control and administration of our institutions." Reinert noted the deluge of supportive letters he had received after the announcement he made in January of that year establishing a new independent board of trustees at Saint Louis University. He concluded, "It is clear that dominance by religious will be replaced, not typically by total turn-over to lay control, but by shared responsibility by religious and laity in Catholic higher education."[4]

The pressure for change was growing. In periodicals such as *America* and *Commonweal,* critics such as Neil G. Mc-Cluskey, S.J., and Andrew Greeley insisted on the need to change the relationship of the colleges to the religious communities if the standards of academic excellence, widely discussed since Msgr. John Tracy Ellis' challenge issued in 1955, were to be attained.[5] McCluskey wrote, for example, in March 1967, that the basic need of Catholic colleges and universities was to recognize that the governance of higher education rested on a different base of authority from that of a religious community. To him, this and not finances was the fundamental problem: "A blank check . . . would not solve problems like the dominance of religious orders, reliance on old-world traditions, amateurish administration, short-sighted financial policies, confusion between pastoral and academic areas, insulation from the main stream of contemporary thought, lack of definition of purpose."[6]

Father Greeley headed a 1966 study undertaken by the National Opinion Research Center to study the changes occurring in Catholic colleges. Referring to that ongoing work, Greeley wrote: "It became clear that the basic problem facing the Catholic schools was a rationalization of the relationship between the college and the religious community. The norms, values and administrative styles governing a religious community, however proper (or improper) they may be for the community, are simply not appropriate for a higher educational institution in American society."[7]

These commentators were calling for a revolution in the life of Catholic colleges. It was not a small matter. To understand the significance of what was being demanded we

must first examine the depth and strength of the fundamental relationship which had characterized life at these
institutions. What was at stake when a change in governance was proposed? How deep were the roots of the college
in the religious mission of the community? How dramatic would be the consequences of allowing independent
boards, composed of religious and lay members, to govern
the institutions?

The Catholic college, begun as a form of direct apostolic
service to the Catholic community, was the place where
the religious exercised their vocation. It was also, in most
cases, a source of religious vocations to the order, and its
raison d'être was closely identified with the church's concern for the faith of its young people. American secular universities were often viewed as hostile to religious faith, and
parents, teachers, and bishops collaborated in supporting
alternative institutions sponsored by religious communities
where young Catholic men and women could receive an
education in secular studies within a cultural and spiritual
environment that was Catholic.[8] While the colleges generally welcomed lay faculty and staff as needed—in some
instances they were in the majority—it was clear that the
religious were "in charge," and the environment thus created reflected their own community life style.

This dominance by the community was not accidental
but was even perceived as essential. One Mother General, writing to a provincial council about appointments,
expressed the request that the First Councillor of the
local community not be the president of the college, so
that "it will be clear that the convent runs the college
and not vice versa." Another General Superior wrote from
Rome expressing approval for the concept of an independent board of trustees because, he felt, "some religious

were more committed to the university than to the religious community." Such recognition on the part of major superiors of the intense feeling that religious, both individually and collectively, had for the college hints at the pain that would be experienced in trying to separate them from one another.

When one woman religious left her community after the college of which she was president had opted for a status as a "secular" institution, she reportedly said that her decision was based on the fact that she had entered the community for the apostolate of that institution and now it was no longer possible. To see one's vocation in terms of participation in the mission of the church was often a major reason for entering religious life. Unfortunately, the attachment to that mission in a particular college which was "owned and operated" by the religious community made the separation of the two organizations life-threatening in a personal spiritual sense.

Even for those religious with a broader vision of their mission, the assignment to higher studies and to teaching and/or administration in "the college" was the way they carried out their vow of obedience. Although they recognized the authority of the deans and presidents over them insofar as faculty duties were concerned, they nevertheless knew that behind the decisions of the president lay the very real authority of their religious superior. Indeed the superior was very often the president as well. In the seven institutions that I have studied in detail, all except the College of New Rochelle and Saint Michael's had one person serving in both capacities, and that seems to have been the prevailing pattern in Catholic higher education until the 1960s. In everyday life it was often hard to know where one authority left off and another began.

One of the difficulties that resulted from this dual role was that since the term of office for a religious superior was canonically set for six years, the president also had to be replaced every six years. The two offices were separated at Notre Dame in 1958, at Mundelein in 1963, and at Fordham in 1967. Even when there were two separate offices, some problems remained. The authority of the superior of the religious community was clear. Together with his or her council, the local, provincial, or general superior made decisions, borrowed the needed funds for the university, requested permissions from higher canonical superiors for unusual expenditures, conferred with the local bishop, and played a decisive role in the selection of the president and other officers of the college. Naturally, all of the members of the community who served in the university were accountable to the superior and sometimes felt at a disadvantage in dealing with lay colleagues because of that relationship. On the other hand, the president often found that members of the religious community took faculty or administration business directly to the superior.

A reading of the minutes of local and provincial councils in the years prior to the transition to independent boards makes abundantly clear that, year by year, the affairs of the college or university were becoming more and more complex. Not only the rapid growth of the institution but also the burgeoning relationships with federal and state agencies created whole new areas of responsibility for those making decisions for the institution. In addition, the change in the composition of the faculties meant that religious superiors were trying to deal with needs of lay faculty, men and women not under their jurisdiction in the same way as religious faculty. As the lay faculty began articulating their concerns about salaries, benefits, tenure and academic freedom, the councils found it increasingly difficult to make policies that would be fair and equitable. The president's power to construct annual university budgets was limited by the religious authority that had overall control of finances. Refusing to grant tenure was sometimes a statement about unacceptable behavior on the part of a faculty member according to the judgment of the religious authorities rather than faculty peers. The fact that all such decisions were made "in council" meant that rumors abounded and actual reasons were scarcely ever known.

This closely interconnected system was now threatened by those who perceived it as having a negative impact on Catholic higher education's move into mainstream American life. How long would it take to separate the two constituent members: college and community? And how would this separation be effected?

A first step in the process concerned finances. Many communities, sometimes at the behest of regional accrediting agencies, had begun in the 1950s to separate the financial records of the community from those of its institutions and to clarify ownership of property. For example, in 1956 the visiting accreditation team from the Middle States Association of Colleges and Secondary Schools recommended that the College of New Rochelle seek a transfer of ownership of the campus (buildings as well as grounds) from the Ursuline Convent of St. Teresa to the corporation of the College of New Rochelle. The two corporations had existed side by side since the founding of the college in 1904, but all of the properties had been registered in the name of the convent corporation. Now, Middle States pointed out that the college, as a separate corporation, should own its own assets. At a meeting of the council of the community on October 23, 1958, all the assets of the St. Teresa corporation (except for the dowries of the nuns) were transferred to the College of New Rochelle corporation.[9]

In other cases, e.g., Saint Louis, Notre Dame, and Trinity College in Washington, D.C., the single corporation that existed was that of the university or college and it owned all the assets. Eventually in many colleges this led to a separate incorporation of the local religious community and a division of properties, but in others the community did not seek separate incorporation and so continued in a dependent position vis à vis the college. Some colleges effected no transfer of ownership and instead, signed agreements with the communities for long-term leases, shared use of buildings, and shared costs for lawn care, snow removal, repairs, and alterations to buildings.

The "separation" in terms of physical properties was far from complete by the 1960s, but it was well underway. The major "separation" that was still needed was that of government. The community's commitment to the institution, its legal control of it, the personal attachment of individual religious to the mission of the college, and the laity's respect and admiration for the community's leadership role in the institution had not yet been questioned. As indicated above, some critics were beginning to suggest that "leadership" of the community might not require control. The difficulties experienced in subsequent years are truly comparable to those of a couple opting for a "separation" but not a "divorce." What did the words imply? In a way, the ambiguity that has existed in the conversation about Catholic colleges and universities since the 1960s stems from this basic unresolved question: once the college was no longer under the control of the religious community and its property was no longer regarded as church property, how was it to be "Catholic" and furthermore, how was it to be Jesuit, Holy Cross, or Mercy? While the separation of assets was perceived by many religious as simply a compliance with legal and fiscal practices, they were deeply and emotionally affected by the transfer of governing authority to a board of trustees not controlled by their religious community, and therefore not "theirs." In some instances, this reaction remained unstated until years later, but oral testimony suggests that it was a reality. One can still occasionally hear voices that express anger or sadness that "their" college was "given away."

And yet several realities had to be recognized. The tension involved in managing the complex life of the university in mid-twentieth century was aggravated by the loss of capable and committed members of the sponsoring religious community. It was during these very years that a significant exodus of priests, brothers, and sisters from religious life occurred. From 1966 to 1969 an estimated 3,413 men resigned from the priesthood. During the same period the number of sisters in the United States began a steady descent from 181,421 in 1966 to 126,517 by 1980.[10] While we do not know how many of those who left were engaged in Catholic higher education, it is clear that the religious orders had to reset priorities and reassign personnel. Even more significant than simply the decrease in the numbers from which to draw faculty or administrators was the change in the general climate of religious life, which now became, in many ways, anti-authority and anti-institutional. Many who wanted to continue teaching in Catholic colleges and universities also wanted the community to "divest itself" of institutional ownership or control. They sometimes spoke of this as a response to the Vatican II document on religious life in which a call to evangelical poverty was renewed. At the same time, the loss of religious faculty and staff personnel added to the financial worries of the president, since the custom of "contributed services" had provided a large share of the institutional revenue. While some religious communities continued to give contributed services, others could no longer afford to do so. The obvious answer seemed to be greater involvement of the laity in fund-raising, and to encourage this, presidents hoped to give such laymen more authority over the spending of the funds raised. Transfer of governance was the way to do that, but was such a divestiture acceptable from the community's point of view? Was it even canonically legal?

Rev. John McGrath, a canonist at The Catholic University of America, provided the necessary rationale to justify it.[11] In his view, institutions that served a public interest such as education and health had historically been entrusted to special civil corporations set up for that purpose. Gifts to those institutions were meant for the promotion of the work of the college or hospital and thus were not gifts to the church. Consequently, they did not become ecclesiastical property. He examined the canon law in this regard and concluded that properties acquired after the incorporation of the institution were to be held "in trust" by the legally appointed designees. The "trustees" governed the institution and administered its resources, while it was the corporation which "owned" the assets. Hence, whether the boards were composed of lay or religious members, the college did not "belong" to the religious community, and, according to McGrath, it was incorrect to speak of the property as church property.

We will examine McGrath's argument in more detail in chapter 3 of this study, but here it is important to recognize the support that it gave to those who sought to have the college authorities manage their own affairs without constraint from religious communities. It meant an end to permissions sought for new lawn mowers as well as new buildings. It satisfied the religious who interpreted the Vatican II documents as demanding a more obvious "poverty" than that shown by large institutional complexes "owned" by religious communities. The McGrath interpretation would make it possible for the administrators to do long-range planning, develop faculty salary scales, and carry out many other managerial tasks without worrying about whether their superiors would approve. Independent governing boards of trustees would become the guardians of the college assets, and they would not be hampered by the needs of the community's other apostolates or the ordinary costs of housing, feeding, and educating community members. This separation would mean that only the interests of the institution would be considered as college leaders prepared budgets and evaluated plans for future expansion.

According to a study of 134 Catholic colleges and universities done at the University of Pennsylvania by Dr. Martin Stamm in 1979, based on 1977 data, about 60 percent reported that they had created independent "unicameral" lay/religious boards of trustees and that the institution was no longer governed by the local or provincial council.[12] Most of the others had increased the presence of lay persons on their boards but had kept some "reserved powers" for the religious authority. The separation of college from community, whether in whole or in part, was now a reality.

The first question that comes to mind is, how did this widespread change in governance occur in so many different places in such a short period of time—just one decade? Secondly, what was the national context of higher education within which Catholic colleges made such drastic changes? Thirdly, what was the historical governing structure in most Catholic colleges and universities prior to this time? Finally, what forces inherent in this structure pushed toward change?

1. The Rapid Pace of Change

The first step in the process had been taken when the financial administration of the college was separated from that of the community. As the presidents worked at this separation, they soon realized the value of having at hand many lay advisors with competence in fiscal and legal affairs. The next logical step was to expand the role of these advisors in the management of the institution, giving them decision-making authority over all its affairs. An additional consideration was the urging by Vatican Council II to recognize the special competence of the laity in "secular" matters. The documents of Vatican II were just being disseminated, and the ecclesial encouragement to increasing the role and responsibility of the laity in church institutions was the perfect complement to many other reasons expressed by the presidents.

According to the recollections of Fathers Hesburgh and Reinert,[13] for example, the role of the laity was a major motive for the steps taken to change governance structure. However, many who hesitated to support lay governance seriously questioned the quality and Catholic commitment of lay persons who would be willing to undertake the work of a true board of trustees.

In fact, many of the first lay trustees for the new boards came from the existing cadre of highly qualified lay advisory trustees. Moreover, the response of lay persons to the invitation to assume greater responsibilities was wholehearted dedication to the mission of the institution and the well-being of the religious community. The theological reasons for the new role were not the dominant factor. In the recollections of Edmund Stephan and Daniel Schlafly,[14] the first chairs of new independent boards at Notre Dame and Saint Louis, they wanted to do whatever "Father" thought would ensure a great future for the university and were willing to assume the responsibilities called for by Vatican II, but they were not terribly concerned about ecclesiological recognition of their status. In assuming responsibility for governance, they were very clear in their determination that the university should remain "Holy Cross" or "Jesuit" as well as "Catholic." They saw the new mode of organization not as a repudiation of those religious communities, but as a necessity if the universities were to become as "great" as their presidents envisioned. They also knew this would take significant resources and were willing to lead a crusade that would bring other laymen on board.

The same dedication to the college mission and its founding community, and the willingness to "help Father or Sister," characterized the attitude of lay advisors at other colleges and gave tremendous support to the presidential project in hand. However, it is important to note that the initiative for independent boards was all on the side of the administrators and their religious communities; there is no evidence of a seizure of power by lay people. Indeed many of them seemed not to be fully conscious of the meaning of the independent trusteeship which was now offered to them or of the complex reasons that motivated the presidents.

Another important factor contributing to the speed with which laicization of the boards was accomplished was the well-developed network among the presidents of many colleges and universities. They were in constant contact with each other and with certain other key leaders, both inside the universities and the religious communities and in national higher education circles and the legal profession. The annual meetings of the National Catholic Educational Association College and University Department furnished an ongoing opportunity for the presidents to exchange ideas. A new cohesiveness was provided in 1965 through the establishment of a full-time office for this department of NCEA,[15] and its new Executive Director, Father Clarence Friedman, gave full support to the movement toward lay boards. The NCEA *College Newsletter* in these years took on the important mission of communicating new developments regarding governance. The agenda for the annual meetings indicate a growing consensus about the need for leaders of Catholic institutions to project a more "independent" image to their colleagues in higher education, i.e., an "independence" from church control.

Father Friedman quickly became a respected member of the higher education community in Washington. He attended board meetings of the Association of American Colleges, where he developed contacts with leaders in other sectors of private higher education, especially those in church-related colleges. AAC had originally opposed the move toward seeking state or federal funds for private colleges out of a fear that such dependence would lead to governmental control and possibly even a Ministry of Education. In 1958, however, AAC reversed its position. Fearful of being left out when funds were distributed, it urged its members to apply for available grants.[16] By 1965 when Friedman took his place at the higher education table, the precedent had already been set by the private colleges. Friedman urged Catholic colleges to study eligibility requirements for both foundation and state funding opportunities and to adapt in such necessary ways as to meet the criteria. Once this move was made, the need for lay trustees with contacts in the corporate and political worlds was self-evident.

The presidents of the twenty-eight Jesuit colleges were also strengthening their collaboration and moving toward the establishment of the Association of Jesuit Colleges and Universities. By setting up this presidential association in 1970, they minimized the control of the provincials in the area of Jesuit higher education and benefited directly from the experience of Paul Reinert, who was clearly the leader among them.[17]

An indication of the developing network of support among the presidents of Catholic colleges and universities is the fact that the same names appear as participants in all the meetings that were being held during these years on the topic of new-style boards: Paul Reinert, Theodore Hesburgh, Ann Ida Gannon, Jacqueline Grennan, Earl McGrath, John McGrath, Gerald Dupont, Leo McLaughlin, Laurence McGinley, Michael Walsh, John Walsh, Andrew Greeley, John Tracy Ellis, Robert Henle, and Neil McCluskey. From correspondence files it is also evident that they sought and received information from one another on the topic of governance and that their legal counsels consulted one another.[18]

We can say, then, that the creation of independent boards of trustees was an idea whose time had come, that the requisite leadership was at hand, and that both ideological support and financial necessity promoted its speedy acceptance.

2. National Context: State of Boards of Control

Catholic colleges and universities were not alone in rethinking the role of trustees and governance. Many other institutions were reorganizing existing boards of trustees and giving more prominence to their role and responsibilities. Although the Association of Governing Boards had been founded in 1921, it only gained national identity in the late 1950s. At first it was an association of trustees of public institutions, admitting private colleges only in the 1960s. A review of the publication *AGB Reports* from 1964 to 1972, the years when AGB moved into visible leadership in the area of trusteeship, testifies to the increasing complexity of higher education which was demanding new structures of governance. In 1965 AGB issued a reprint of the Middle States Association of Colleges and Secondary Schools' 1957 document entitled "Functions of Boards of Trustees in Higher Education" and distributed it to its members. Today the advice given in this booklet seems elementary, because most of it became common practice over the next thirty years. It identifies three areas of trustee responsibility: institutional policy, presidential relations, and financial resources. Trustees, it points out, represent "the founders, the benefactors, and the public." In speaking of financial resources, mention is made of the "contributed services" of religious, which are the equivalent of significant endowments. (As noted above, the loss of such services worried the presidents in the late sixties.) For private institutions as a whole, gifts and endowments were the most common sources of funding. The importance of trustees is underscored: "Trustees, although they are not usually themselves educators, control American higher education."[19]

Concern about governing boards was also evident on the state level, since education was still regarded as a state rather than a federal responsibility. For example, in February 1966 the Regents in New York State appointed a special committee, chaired by President James Perkins of Cornell University, to assess educational leadership in the state.

The Perkins Committee report[20] made several recommendations, among them the need to professionalize the role of trustees, a need strongly felt by most of the institutions in the state. Several specific actions were suggested: a nominating process for the selection of trustees; a responsible way of selecting and monitoring the president; the development of various committees of the board of trustees; avoidance of any contact with other administrators that would bypass the president. That these trustee responsibilities, so taken for granted today, would have been spelled out in detail by a blue-ribbon committee of New York State, a state with the reputation of having the most highly developed system of higher education in the country, suggests to us that Catholic colleges were not so far behind their colleagues in developing the art of trusteeship. The presidents of the Catholic institutions in New York quoted from this report in order to convince others of the need to update their governmental structures and remove the last vestige of community control over such things as appointment of the president and the trustees.

Another report—this one under the auspices of the Danforth Foundation—was issued in 1965 and dealt with the 817 American church-related colleges. Although the report was concerned primarily with the religious character of these institutions, it called attention to the special problems in Roman Catholic colleges due to the composition and authority of their boards and lay-religious faculty relationships.[21] The Danforth study helped the Catholic colleges by focusing on the elements in the relationship between college and church which were seen as determinative of the college's religious character: composition of boards; ownership and legal relationship; financial support; acceptance of denominational standards on the use of the name; educational aims; and selection of faculty and administration. As the Catholic colleges moved to independent boards, it would be important for them to be aware of these elements, taking account of the way in which they had existed in the historic relationship of college to religious community, and searching for ways to retain their Catholic character without the legal underpinnings that once assured it.

3. Governance at Catholic Colleges and Universities

These various studies indicated the general need in American higher education of the period for a reform in the governing structures of the institutions. Even in those universities that were not church-related, the trustees were slow to understand and accept their real responsibility for the institution. However, they did not have the problem of dual authority structures which existed in Catholic colleges and also in some other church-related institutions. The latter, related to church bodies rather than to religious communities, often had a greater financial dependence on the particular church's convention or judicature than did the Catholic colleges. It was also true that many of them had a tradition of church body's appointment of trustees and approval of program of studies.

However, in the present study we are concerned only with Roman Catholic colleges, and it will be useful to examine in detail their governance structures prior to the introduction of lay boards. For this, let us consider the Proceedings of a 1947 workshop held at The Catholic University of America. The leader of the workshop, Rev. Alcuin W. Tasch, described the common structures of governance, pointing out that over 90 percent of the colleges were under the direct control of religious orders. "They are private institutions and in their internal organization and administration enjoy complete autonomy according to the provisions of their respective constitutions and statutes."[22] There was no uniform mode of governance but, according to Tasch, there were seven characteristic ways that religious orders structured the governance of their institutions:

1. The Religious Corporation is the parent corporation and owns the property and facilities used by the college;
2. There is one Corporation, the Religious one, and it conducts the institution as one of its activities;
3. The Religious Corporation or community, in all cases, furnishes most of the personnel, administration, and faculty for the college;
4. Religious Superiors constitute the board of trustees, either entirely or in majority ratio;
5. Religious Superiors exercise their canonical prerogative of the disposition of their subjects in the matter of appointments;
6. Religious Corporations and/or religious superiors exercise certain financial controls below the limits set by Canon Law for the Holy See;
7. The president may also be the religious superior, local or major.[23]

Tasch pointed out that in order to have legal status in the United States, religious communities and ecclesiastical authorities regularly obtained a corporation charter, thereby acquiring a separate, juridic personality, and included in the charter might be the right to engage in higher education. In some cases, religious communities organized a second corporation for the college. According to Tasch, such a separate corporation required authorization in accordance

with religious statutes. "Canon law and the religious constitutions also contain certain restrictive provisions in the
matter of final internal control."[24] In 1947 most boards had
no lay members, although Tasch pointed out that such lay
representation was rapidly gaining favor among women's
colleges.

The dual authority of the canon and civil law codes, as
described in the the 1947 workshop, did not change for two
decades. The later work of Edward Stanford, O.S.A.,[25] is
based on this accepted reality. He upheld the importance
of "control" remaining with the religious community, although he saw the need for a civil charter for the college
separate from that of the religious community lest the
community bear civil liability beyond its means. Stanford's
main concern was that there be clarity about the functions of the two corporations and their distinctive boards.
"Certainly the board of trustees must be so constituted that
there can be no question about the control of the college
being vested in the Religious Community which assures its
existence and continued operation. This means that at least
a majority of the board members must also be members of
the Religious Community."[26] Stanford also thought that
the immediate major religious superior should be the chair
of the college board. The emphasis on "control" that is
so evident in Stanford's exposition was precisely the factor
that was already losing support as his work was being published in 1965.

In explaining his views at that time, of course, Stanford
did not yet have access to the Vatican II documents which
would suggest a more equitable sharing of power with the
laity. Nor did he live to experience the changed climate in
the wake of the *Horace Mann* decision, a decision that will
be treated at length in chapter 3. Had it not been for Stan-

ford's untimely death in 1967, he may well have revised some of his thinking, but at the time of his writing he was not ready to give up the concept of "control."

Given the Tasch and Stanford prescriptions, we can better understand the findings of the Ford-Roy study discussed earlier. In answer to the questions on governance it was concern over the role of religious orders that was central. The authors summarized the situation: "In the past two or three decades, there has been a tremendous growth in the numbers of laymen engaged in full-time work in Catholic colleges and universities. But, until quite recently, the religious have exercised the leadership and control with the laymen 'filling in' necessary gaps."[27]

According to the Ford-Roy report, until very recently most institutions were governed by boards of trustees composed exclusively of members of the religious order. Often these persons were administrators of the college, and they were joined by officers of the general provincial administration. The report discusses the advantages and disadvantages of the movement toward a change in the locus of governing authority: among the former, the additional expertise and perspective of lay people and the broader base for financial assistance; among the latter, the scarcity of well-informed lay people for the role of trustee and the fear that the Catholic identity of the institution will become less clear and that some segments of the public will see the move as secularization.

The Ford-Roy study enabled the presidents, and enables us today, to put the decisions that were being made into a context of factual data about the institutions—size, students, faculty, facilities, etc.—and about the concerns uppermost in the minds of the presidents. Enrollments were going up, and it seemed the right moment to jump into the mainstream of American higher education, but to do that would require better governance and greater funding.

Further data on the composition of current boards of trustees was gathered by two other members of the "network" we have described: Rev. Gerald E. Dupont, S.S.E., president of Saint Michael's College, and Dr. Earl J. McGrath, director of the Institute of Higher Education at Teachers' College of Columbia University. Early in 1967 they circulated a questionnaire to 339 Catholic institutions regarding their boards and received a 75 percent response, itself indicative of the relevance of the topic. Removing the seminaries from the data gathered, McGrath and Dupont did their analysis on the 167 participants who represented two-year and four-year colleges and universities educating lay men and women.[28] According to the McGrath-Dupont study, 31 percent of these institutions had laymen (*sic*) on their boards of control prior to 1966. They note that a few had lay trustees from their foundation: Fordham (1842), Villanova (1846), Seton Hall (1856), Manhattan (1863), College of St. Thomas (1885), and St. Francis, Brooklyn (1889). This author has discovered a few more: LaSalle, College of New Rochelle, and the University of Portland. However, historical study is complicated by the fact that in most of these cases, whatever direct role in decision-making was played by these early lay trustees, governance by the mid-twentieth century was clearly the exclusive preserve of the religious community. The McGrath-Dupont study notes that only eighteen Catholic colleges and universities, 11 percent of those in the study, had lay members on their boards in 1940. Rapid increase in the number of colleges with lay trustees from 1941 to 1965 raised the 1966 figure to 31 percent and, in the eighteen months following the *Horace Mann* decision, that figure grew to 45 percent.[29]

In retrospect we can say that the *Horace Mann* decision, which declared two Maryland Catholic colleges ineligible for federal grants because they were judged to be "sectarian," hastened the move to reorganize boards.[30] Although the Maryland Court of Appeals decision only had legal authority within the state, and the Supreme Court refused to take the case on appeal, the criteria that had been used in this case to determine eligibility for federal construction funds were to form the parameters of court cases and legislative judgments about the church-state issues involved in the financing of private higher education. The questions raised about the composition of boards penetrated the consciousness of presidents and lawyers alike, and they saw a new urgency in reforming their boards. As we shall see later on, these same questions were raised in the *Tilton* case in Connecticut in the next year, and were included in the preparatory materials for application for New York State grants to private higher education known as Bundy money. The consequences of this will be dealt with at length in the section on Fordham in chapter 2 and also in chapter 3.

In the light of these studies and the adverse legal decisions of 1966–68, it is not surprising that the movement toward independent boards gained momentum. The Perkins study, referred to above, had already given pause to the leaders of Catholic colleges, suggesting as it did that Catholic colleges constituted a sort of subgroup with a form of government distinct from that of most private institutions and intimately connected to religious communities. The McGrath-Dupont survey provided comparative data on Catholic colleges and interpreted them as pointing the way to new models of shared governance that would provide independence for colleges and universities. Fear that their colleges would be discriminated against in the programs of federal and state assistance to private higher education intensified the presidents' desire to change the government of their institutions.

This then was the "state of the art" of trusteeship in Catholic colleges and universities in the latter half of the 1960s. In retrospect, it appears to have been the right moment because all the elements were present for a revolutionary change: there was unusually strong leadership among the presidents, a movement toward reform of boards of trustees in the wider American higher education community, studies which focused attention on some perceived weaknesses, a growing consciousness in the Catholic colleges that they were perceived as a subgroup in higher education bearing the burden of proof in the face of their secular counterparts, an openness to change on the part of religious superiors, a growing anxiety about funding, and an ecclesial revolution in the way some canonists thought about lay persons and about the binding force of canon law with regard to property entrusted to civil corporations.

The teachings of Vatican II on the role of laity were increasingly cited as the reason for independent boards when the decision had to be explained to alumnae/i, parents, donors, and religious communities. The extent to which the religious communities accepted this reason undoubtedly varied. As a matter of fact, the communities were often not informed about the transfer of power until after it was accomplished. When the proposals were debated openly as, for example, at the provincial chapter held at Notre Dame in January 1967 or in the faculty meetings presided over by Sister Ann Ida at Mundelein, many explanations were given for the suggested changes, and differences of opinion were voiced and recorded. In other cases, it is hard to discover just how much the community knew of

RETIREMENT
PLANNING
FOR EVERY
LIFE STAGE

FREE
GUIDE
See other
side

BUSINESS REPLY MAIL
FIRST-CLASS MAIL   PERMIT NO. 22   TAMPA FL

POSTAGE WILL BE PAID BY ADDRESSEE

Money

PO BOX 61790
TAMPA FL 33661-1790

NO POSTAGE
NECESSARY
IF MAILED
IN THE
UNITED STATES

the radical shift in power that was occurring. Many religious have told this author that the "grassroots" knew very little about it all. Annals of the community at the College of New Rochelle make no mention of the transfer of property to the college corporation in 1958 or of the revision of the bylaws in 1964 which recognized the complete independence of the board of trustees, a predominantly lay group.[31]

As one would expect, the arguments used to pursuade each constituency varied, and the presidents were very skilled at adapting their presentations to different audiences. In their search for wide support, they undoubtedly looked, as the Middle States document on the functions of trustees had advised, "to tradition, the nature of the sponsoring group, the hopes, desires, and expectations of the constituency to be served, the point of view of the particular academic community, and practical educational considerations among them." What Middle States had urged was not a univocal model of a board but rather that the board, however composed of lay or religious members, should have the wisdom and authority to make decisions for the college.

What may surprise us as we examine the changes made at a sampling of Catholic universities and colleges is that they opted for more radical adjustments than had been proposed by the accrediting agencies, the canon lawyers, or most of their consultants. The questions now before us are Why? and How? To answer these questions we must look at the specific cases, because the institutions and communities had different reasons for their decisions and used various processes to effect the transfer of governance to independent boards.

TWO

Independence

THE PROCESS OF LAICIZATION

The significant actions taken by Catholic institutions of higher learning in the late 1960s pose dramatic questions for the historian. They deal with causality, motivation, and human decision. Several in particular stand out: Why did it seem opportune to shift control of the institution from the religious community to an independent board of trustees? What moved the lay men and women to accept such new responsibilities? Why were the religious willing to give up control of their apostolic mission? What fears were expressed by those who opposed this action? Was it really a result of the theological rethinking of the role of the laity in the church as expressed by Vatican Council II?

The answers to these questions are not univocal. To illustrate the expansion of the role of lay persons in the governing authority of Catholic colleges, I will examine the process followed in seven institutions. Each of the seven will offer unique insights about the process of transferring governing authority to a board independent of the religious authority of the sponsoring community. Nevertheless, keeping in mind the differences among them, I will suggest some commonalities, many of which reflect the basic relationship between the religious community and the college or university it founded. These seven institutions gave witness to a unity of purpose even as they adopted diverse methods of laicization.

The College of New Rochelle

The history of governance at the College of New Rochelle is of special interest because it was not typical of
women's colleges, nor does it resemble the history of the
men's colleges studied here.[1] Its president in 1964–66, when
the reorganization occurred, was not part of the network of
leaders described in chapter 1, although its legal counsel
was. Its foundress was Mother Irene Gill, an Ursuline nun,
but the original 1904 charter committed the college to the
care of a board of ten persons, one cleric and nine lay
men. In subsequent years the membership of this governing
board grew to seventeen elected men. These men were extremely important as advisors and legal spokesmen, yet they
seemed to take decisions only after informal consultation
with the superior of the Ursuline community. Even the Executive Committee of the board, set up in 1909, was com-
prised of seven lay men—no Ursulines. As early as 1918 the
board discussed the process to be followed for the choice of
a new president and decided by themselves to proceed "only
after consultation with the faculty." In planning for the in-
auguration of the new president, the board again decided
that it must first consult the faculty, composed at this
time mostly of lay men. Thus the early history of the college shows an unusual reliance of the nuns on their lay colleagues.[2] By 1924 there were twenty-three lay trustees, all
men. In 1928 the board added its first woman trustee, a lay
alumna; this was done at Mother Irene's suggestion, based
on information she had received from AAC that women's
colleges ought to have some women trustees.

It was only in 1942 that Ursulines became trustees. In
1945 the Executive Committee consisted of four Ursulines and the president of the college, Msgr. Francis Walsh.
In the bylaws of 1947 the Executive Committee was desig-

nated as: a delegate of the archbishop, the superior of the Ursuline community at the college, and three other Ursuline trustees. In 1954 it was changed to consist of the superior and four other Ursulines elected annually by the board. This group of five from that time on was identical with the council of the local community.

While this description of the changes in the role of the Ursulines in the governance of the college may seem overly meticulous, it is important because it demonstrates a movement away from the earlier recognition of the importance of the lay trustees. It also illustrates the tightening of the bonds between the community and "its" college. Control of the legal board through an exclusively Ursuline Executive Committee gave the community leaders a free hand in decisions for the next decade.

The new dominance by the Ursulines can be explained, in part, by a renewal of their own tradition as educators, traceable to the influence of Mother St. Jean Martin, Mother General from 1926 to 1959 and a resident in the United States during World War II. Her vision of Ursuline education required the Ursulines to be in a position of control. While students and faculty had never doubted that, in spite of the legal authority of the lay trustees, the Ursulines were "in charge," the governing role that they played was to become more overt. The mission of the college had always been described in terms of the Ursuline tradition, i.e., as the education of Catholic young women for lives of service to the church and society. However in the 1950s the new lay faculty members were given copies of a basic text written by the Mother General, entitled *Ursuline Method of Education,* and faculty study days were often devoted to a consideration of that method and its relevance to the twentieth century.

In 1950 the college received its first Ursuline president. Previously, the presidents had been priests selected by the board after consultation with the cardinal and the local superior. These priest-presidents, however, came to campus infrequently. The real CEO was the dean, an Ursuline nun. The cardinal did not sit on the board of trustees, but he did have the privilege of delegating a priest to represent him on the board.[3]

In 1958, as described in chapter 1, the assets of the convent corporation were transferred to the college corporation. This was done in compliance with a recommendation of the Middle States Association. It was seen as a simple change in administration which would not in any way affect the Ursuline commitment to the work of the college. It would soon become clear, however, that the whole relationship of the college to the religious community was in need of thoughtful examination. Questions of ownership, control, and governance came to the fore at faculty meetings, where decisions of the administration were often questioned, and at trustee meetings, where the complex nature of higher education was becoming ever more clear.

Minutes of the board of trustees between 1957 and 1964 reflect growing tensions between lay and clerical faculty[4] and record the gradual movement of administrators and faculty toward independence from religious authorities. The appointment of three different Ursuline presidents in 1957, 1961, and 1963 by the provincial government, with election by the board of trustees a foregone conclusion, highlighted the problem of continuity in administration if presidential appointments were left to the discretion of religious superiors. It also demonstrated the need for different structures of accountability. Work began on a reorganization of the board, and in 1964 a draft of new bylaws made it clear that no religious authority lay above the legal board; however, the draft did provide for *ex officio* membership on the board of the provincial and the local superior. But when the final draft of the bylaws was approved in September 1966, this provision was eliminated from the bylaws and became simply a "commentary," which stated that the provincial and the local superior would always be on the ballot for election as trustees. Even this was repealed in 1969, after it appeared (without authorization) in the bylaws as printed in the faculty handbook and aroused some negative faculty response.

The bylaws of 1966 increased the number of trustees, contained no minimum number of Ursulines to be elected, and had no *ex officio* members except the president of the college. The Executive Committee, elected by the board, was composed of both lay and religious and could be chaired by a lay person. This was a significant change, for although the chair of the board had been a layman up until 1956 (one serving in that position from 1943 to 1956), this had been changed in 1957 when the superior became *ex officio* chair of the board, and the Ursuline council of St. Teresa's community had, in practice, become the Executive Committee of the board, also chaired by the superior. However until 1961 the board meetings were in fact chaired by the vice chair, Msgr. Walsh. No explanation other than clerical prerogative is offered for this.

In 1960 a petition to raise the number of trustees from ten to twenty-five had been submitted to and approved by Albany. Consequently, during the 1960s several more lay persons as well as more Ursulines were added to the board. Only after 1966, however, were lay members elected to the Executive Committee. At the same time, an agreement was made by which the nuns on the faculty were given rank and salary comparable to lay colleagues, and the community received actual salaries for their services. It was then up to the community to determine the amount of the "gift" to be made to the college. TIAA and other benefits were to be phased in as soon as possible.

In all of the discussions leading up to the 1966 bylaws, there is no suggestion of New Rochelle becoming a "secular" college or of changing the college's image as Catholic and Ursuline. The spirit of the negotiations was one of professionalization and partnership between the nuns and their colleagues, whether on the faculty or the board of trustees. An attempt to define this relationship was made by a joint committee of the board and the Ursulines in 1969–70, but in the end, the draft agreement was tabled indefinitely; the community thought it best not to put such an agreement in writing at the time. The question of the nuns' future residence facilities was not resolved until 1971, when an adjustment of the property which had been transferred in 1958 was negotiated.[5]

All of this seems to have happened with little public announcement or attention. Since there had always been lay trustees, it did not seem like a revolution, and since the two corporations had existed from the beginning, there was no major decision about "separate incorporation" to be made. Without any prescription in the bylaws of 1966, the Ursulines have continued to constitute about one-fifth of the board and, except for two years, the college has been headed by an Ursuline president.

There is little doubt that the legal counsel at New Rochelle, Mr. Charles Horgan, was influential in all these changes in governance.[6] Horgan himself was devoted to the college, of which both his sister and his wife were alumnae. His advice was accepted by the leadership in both the college and the community at the time. Horgan, watching the courts as they took up various cases regarding loans to church-related institutions and advising the Jesuits at Fairfield as they prepared for the *Tilton* case, was clearly of the opinion that the separation of college from religious community should be clear and complete. In 1962 he urged that more lay persons be added to the board; in 1963 he recommended having a layman on the Executive Committee. The bylaws of 1966 provided for both recommendations, and in 1966 a layman was elected chair of both the board and the Executive Committee.

Horgan was also an alumnus and associate trustee at the Jesuit College of the Holy Cross in Worcester, Massachusetts. He designed the bylaws for Holy Cross, working from 1967 to 1969 with Rev. Raymond Swords, S.J., president at the time.[7] He later became the first lay chair of the Holy Cross board. As a well-known Catholic layman, Horgan was convincing in his arguments for more meaningful lay responsibility in the governance of Catholic institutions. When President Reinert of Saint Louis University invited the other Jesuit presidents and their legal counselors to a meeting in May 1967 to study lay trusteeship, Charles Horgan was a participant. It is clear from the chronology at New Rochelle that he had already bought into the ideas that Reinert was espousing. He was certainly one of the "network" described in chapter 1, although unfortunately he did not leave extensive correspondence that would document his role. However from the testimony of his colleagues it is safe to assume that he was a significant player. In a paper that he prepared for the board of trustees at New Rochelle in 1966 on the *Horace Mann* case, his acceptance of the McGrath thesis is clear. A former partner of his has pointed out that Horgan was also the attorney for

Manhattanville College, but the direction that its president, Mother Elizabeth McCormack, R.S.C.J., chose—i.e., to be "secular"—was not the one he favored, so his service there was terminated. (The decision made at Manhattanville was similar to that of Webster College, which will be discussed here briefly; the connection Manhattanville had with its founding community, the Religious of the Sacred Heart, was minimal in the years that followed.)

The case of New Rochelle is cited because its history was unique in terms of lay leadership and early acceptance of bylaws setting up a truly independent board. It is also clear that through its legal counsel it was motivated by the decision in the 1966 *Horace Mann* case and by concern about eligibility for any aid that New York State might decide to grant independent institutions of higher education. Although recollections are that relations between the New Rochelle presidents and Fathers Hesburgh and Reinert were ongoing and friendly, the only documented link is the presence of Mr. Horgan at the May 1967 meeting, a year after the college bylaws had become operational. Ironically, New Rochelle, with its independent board, was declared ineligible for the Bundy funding in 1969, whereas Fordham University, with an all-Jesuit board just in the process of rethinking its governance, was declared eligible.

Bundy money was a centerpiece in the transitions in governance made in New York State. The criteria for aid eligibility were issued in August 1968,[8] and from then on, competition to comply was the order of the day. In the first assignment of funds, only three Catholic colleges qualified, and the others all wondered why. According to Ewald Nyquist, Assistant Commissioner of Education, Fordham, Manhattanville, and St. John Fisher were approved because "none of them is now under the control or

direction of a religious denomination or teaches denominational tenets or doctrine. Important departures from the
past have occurred at each institution, with the result that
each has become independent of former ties, both in governance and in teaching."[9] Eventually, after several court
contests, this judgment would also be extended to New
Rochelle and the other Catholic colleges that applied for
Bundy aid in the 1970s and 1980s.

In summary, the College of New Rochelle provides
an example of long-time lay involvement in governance
which, after a period of Ursuline control, culminated in an
independent, predominantly lay board with total governing
authority in 1966. New Rochelle never had a board composed exclusively of the members of the religious community, although the nuns, by composing a majority on the
board and the total membership of the Executive Committee in the 1950s, and by a high degree of moral suasion the
rest of the time, did exercise control over the life of the college until 1966.

In the Midwest at the same time, several Catholic colleges and universities were considering ways of changing
their own structures. At both the University of Notre
Dame and Saint Louis University, plans for moving toward
inclusion of laymen on boards of trustees were in progress
by 1965. But both of them were thrown off balance by an
announcement from a small women's college in Webster
Groves, St. Louis, in January 1967. Unlike the colleges and
universities in this study, Webster College did identify "laicization" with "secularization" but it deserves mention here
because its president's action raised a fundamental issue:
Would lay boards and secularization have to go together?

In November 1966 the sister-president of Webster,
Jacqueline Grennan, S.L., had reached the conclusion that,

the freedom necessary for a first-rate college or university could not be achieved as long as there were any links between it and religious authority. In an address to her faculty she announced that henceforth Webster would be governed by a completely lay board with no ties to the Sisters of Loretto or the Catholic Church. Cardinal Ritter, archbishop of St. Louis, had been asked by the Superior General, Sister Luke Tobin, to secure the necessary permission for the sisters to alienate their property in favor of the lay board. The reasons given to Cardinal Ritter by the General Council were three: (1) the need for increased finances dictated giving fiscal responsibility to the board; (2) since the lay faculty constituted 75 percent of the faculty, administration had become too complex for a religious congregation to handle along with other responsibilities; and (3) there was a lack of qualified sister-personnel to fill administrative and faculty posts. This action was taken after a year's consideration by the sisters and was shared in confidence with the faculty since the canonical permission had not yet been received.[10]

Within months the permission was received, and the public announcement was made on January 11, 1967. In due course, Sister Jacqueline became simply Dr. Grennan. In that capacity she continued as president of Webster. Again, her publicly stated reason was that as a Sister of Loretto she represented the church, and the church could not be responsible for a college or university. It was a contradiction in terms.[11] Quick responses came from other religious women. A full page ad in *The New York Times* communicated the message that the alumnae and students of Marymount-Manhattan were totally committed to the leadership of their president and the religious of the Sacred Heart of Mary. The president of Trinity College in Washington, D.C., Margaret Claydon, S.N.D., issued a statement for the Washington papers saying that Trinity retained strong faith in its mission as a Catholic college. Opinions regarding "Jacqueline" were strong and generally negative among women religious, and with the exception of Manhattanville, Catholic women's colleges did not follow the Webster model of laicization—i.e., a board of trustees exclusively lay and without any special relationship to the founding religious community or to the Catholic church.

Saint Louis University

Across town the January 11 announcement from Webster College created an extremely uncomfortable situation for Rev. Paul Reinert, S.J., president of Saint Louis University. For about two years he had been engaged in discussions with his provincial and Father General Arrupe as well as with the presidents of other Jesuit universities regarding the establishment of a primarily lay governing board for the university.[12] Webster's public announcement of "secular" status as simultaneous with the establishment of a "lay" board led to the possibility of great misunderstanding of Reinert's plans for Saint Louis. Nevertheless, he pressed forward and on January 21, 1967, announced the selection of Daniel Schlafly, an outstanding lay Catholic in St. Louis, as the chair of a newly designed board of trustees. Reinert did take the precaution of asking Cardinal Ritter for a public statement as to the continued "Catholic" and "Jesuit" identity of his institution; this the Cardinal provided in a letter to Father Reinert which was quoted in the news release of January 21. He wrote: "My congratulations to you and those who are working with you on the project for the enlargement of the board of directors. . . . Be assured of my enthusiasm and wholehearted support and approval of this proposal to enlarge your board and to involve laymen in the direction and policy-making responsibilities of the University. It is very much in keeping with the spirit of Vatican Council II." Father Arrupe, Superior General, was also affirming: "I am very happy with the proposed greater collaboration of laymen in the direction of the University." He quoted from the decree on education of the Thirty-first General Congregation of the Society of Jesus which recommended investigation of "the advisability of establishing boards of trustees composed both of Jesuit and lay men."[13]

The process for change at Saint Louis would not mirror that at Webster. It would aim rather to strengthen the Catholic and Jesuit identity of the university precisely by involving notable Catholic lay men and women in the actual governance of the institution. In April when the members of the board were announced, the inclusion of Eunice Kennedy Shriver, Dr. Edmund Pellegrino, and Carroll A. Hochwalt among other outstanding trustees, both Catholic and non-Catholic, indicated the level of support that Father Reinert was seeking. Of the eighteen lay trustees, nine were Catholic and nine were of other faiths but all, according to Reinert, were totally committed to the Jesuit and Catholic future of Saint Louis University. Five of the existing Jesuit board of trustees would carry over to the new board (all of them administrators at Saint Louis) and five other Jesuits were appointed: Raymond Baumhart, John Donohue, Paulinus Forsthoefel, A. A. Lemieux, and David Stanley—all outstanding scholars of the Society. With such a board, Reinert anticipated progress on all fronts.

The decision at Saint Louis had important ramifications for the entire Jesuit cohort of twenty-eight colleges/universities, and the care which was expended to bring them all "on board" sheds light on the very sensitive issues that were involved. Paul Reinert's leadership in Catholic higher education—as evidenced in his many addresses to the NCEA College and University Department and his initiation of the Ford/Roy study mentioned above—gave his decision a special significance for the wider world of higher education. In addition, he was a close collaborator of Rev. Theodore Hesburgh, C.S.C., whose leadership in higher education was recognized both nationally and internationally, and who in 1965 had initiated conversation with his provincial superior and Holy Cross leadership in Rome regarding his vision for a predominantly lay board of trustees at the University of Notre Dame.

In the case of both presidents—Reinert and Hesburgh— remarkable skills of persuasion are evident. In community meetings, provincial chapters, trips to Rome, and personal conversations with superiors on local and provincial levels, they left no stone unturned in the campaign to convince their respective orders of the wisdom of sharing responsibility for the future of their universities with lay people. Both saw an opportunity in the current ecclesial commitment to openness, freedom, and ecumenism for them to join the ranks of American higher education. Ten years earlier John Tracy Ellis had challenged them to pursue intellectual excellence; now they saw a way to secure the freedom and the resources to do it. This goal was one clear answer to the question, Why?

What was the history of the institution led by Paul Reinert? The original civil charter of Saint Louis dated back to 1832 and did not refer specifically to the Jesuits. However from 1832 to 1967 the trustees were Jesuits, numbering thrteen in 1967. There was only one corporation, that of Saint Louis University. According to the constitution of the university, the university operated "under civil law and the canon law of the Catholic Church"; it had a "dual character, the Saint Louis University Corporation which derives its authority in part from its civil charter, as amended, and in part from the canon law of the Catholic Church, as particularized in the Constitutions and Regulations of the Society of Jesus and of the Sacred Congregation of Seminaries and Universities."[14] Further, the constitution of the university specified that as Jesuits the trustees are "personally bound by the restrictions of canon law with regard to the ownership and administration of property as specified in the Constitution and Regulations of the Society of Jesus."[15] It was, no doubt, this clause that later gave rise to Father James O'Connor's suggestion that if the trustees were now to be laymen, something specific needed to be said about canon law and their accountability to it.[16]

According to Father Reinert, conversations about a change in the governance structure began in 1964, and discussions were continual throughout 1964–1966. Two years of meetings, draft documents, commissioned papers, and communication with Rome leave no room to doubt the concern to do everything in accordance with Jesuit protocol. In a confidential memo to the Executive Committee of the board of trustees dated March 21, 1966,[17] Father Reinert shared his vision of a new mode of governance. He outlined the steps to be taken: bylaws that would create an autonomous board of trustees; separate incorporation of the Jesuit community; and a tripartite agreement among the three partners, the province, the local Jesuit community, and the university. In addition, he stressed the desirability of Saint Louis being the first in the field of Catholic universities to accomplish this task. Interestingly, the reasons he put forth did not include any emphasis on the role of the laity in the church, a reason which came to be cited frequently as time went on and which Father Reinert now considers one of major importance. Rather, the discussion in his memo focused on the need to have the outside world take the university seriously, and he saw as an obstacle the continued image of Saint Louis as Jesuit-controlled. The situation was such that the lay advisors did not see themselves as being responsible for the university. However, at this early stage of his thinking, Reinert believed that handing over legal responsibility and the assets of the university to a lay/Jesuit board would require an "indult of alienation" and for that, permission would have to be sought from Rome. He made the point that Hesburgh was already talking to authorities there, so he hoped that permission would be granted to the Jesuits when they requested it.

Reinert, addressing his fellow Jesuits on the Executive Committee, confronted honestly what one of the problems would be: the Jesuits would welcome any plan that increased the involvement of others but would not want to forfeit control of decision-making. "We tend to look for a happy marriage between self-contained control and outside concern and involvement."[18] Reinert argued that simply rearranging the structure of governance would be a subterfuge, and Saint Louis must make a clear break from the current structure. However, by definition, it would remain Catholic and related to the Society of Jesus. Finally, he argued for this change as the only way he saw to obtain the needed financial stability, stressing the role of foundations and the clout that lay trustees would have in approaching them.

Reinert asked the members of the Executive Committee for a response and it was not long in coming. Father Drummund, for example, affirmed the ideas being presented by Reinert and added an emphasis of his own. Asking himself whether or not Jesuits should continue to be involved in higher education, he answered with a strong defense of the intellectual apostolate. Referring to Father Walter Ong's supportive observations on the policy of urging young Jesuits to serve in Jesuit universities, Drummond argued that their role in higher education would be strengthened by this move toward lay responsibility. He pleaded pursuasively for a new way to exercise influence in the academic disciplines in a society that tends to be "secular, fragmented, depersonalized, and dubious about its value base." Students, faculty, and the wider community, he argued, want a Jesuit university that "measures up to leading public institutions in the quality of its academic programs; secondly, they will want it to offer something more and different than such institutions; finally, they will want to have real voice in the way its policies and programs are developed." In his opinion, "the orientation, the value-set, the unifying purpose could have a wider and deeper influence if we Jesuits were precisely not the owners of the University."[19]

Father Trafford Maher responded in a similar vein, arguing that to move out of the "own and operate" mode would bring freedom to Jesuits in their relations with students and faculty, since they would not be burdened with finances and central administration. He even proposed that the president need not be a Jesuit, a point of view not incorporated in the final bylaws.[20] Father Henle suggested that even the language "own and operate" was faulty and should not be used. He urged total separation of the religious community from the university, and argued that the "visitations" from superiors and prefects of studies that were the practice were utterly meaningless.[21]

When Reinert addressed the Society of Jesus General Council and the American provincials in Rome in October 1966, he argued that permission for alienation was unnecessary, on the grounds that the new bylaws would contain a statement binding the trustees to uphold canon law and a provision that amending the bylaws would require a two-thirds vote of the entire board. Given the proposed mix of Jesuits and laymen on the board, a bloc vote by laymen would always fall short of a two-thirds majority by at least one vote. This came to be known as the Jesuit veto power. In a letter to the Missouri provincial, Linus Thro, on October 30, 1966, Father General Arrupe expressed the satisfaction of those who had heard Reinert's ideas on October 8. Arrupe had previously received from Reinert the drafts of new bylaws of August 1, 1966 and September 15, 1966, so he was familiar with the plans and told Thro that he agreed with the direction in which Saint Louis was going.[22]

On December 21, 1966 the Saint Louis board of trustees (i.e., thirteen Jesuits) elected Mr. Daniel Schlafly both as chair of the board and chair of the Executive Committee. During the following months, members of the existing lay advisory board would be invited to membership on the new board of trustees, and the bylaws would be developed with legal counsel. Mr. Schlafly, for his part, was willing to assume this work only if it were clear to Cardinal Ritter and Father Arrupe that his intent was to continue the Catholic and Jesuit mission of the university. In informing him of the board's decision, Reinert wrote: "The move to reorganize its Board contemplated by the University is undoubtedly the most far-reaching decision in our history and will shape our future and that of many other Jesuit, Catholic and other church-related institutions."[23]

The public announcement of the reorganization and the selection of Mr. Schlafly as chair was made on January 21,

1967. Schlafly would serve in that position from 1967 until 1979. In the announcement, Father Reinert focused on the desire to involve all constituencies of the university in achieving its fundamental objectives, and also cited the general movement in the church "to give laymen a greater role." This may mark the first public articulation of a motive that became more pronounced as time went on.

In the months after this announcement, work went forward on the selection of members and the preparation of bylaws. One recurring question involved the reference to canon law. It had been proposed and accepted at a trustee meeting on July 16, 1966 that the bylaws would include the following: "All the members of the Board of Trustees, singly and jointly, bind themselves to the observance not only of the requirements of civil law in the particular jurisdiction in question, but also to all the requirements of canon law—for any type of administrative decision or action that the Board may deem it fit to consider by way of adoption, rejection, or modification."[24] In a letter of December 16, 1966 to Father Marchetti, the executive vice president and secretary to the board, Mr. Thomas V. Connelly, legal counsel to Saint Louis, argued against this proposed bylaw. Connelly saw this provision as very dangerous because it would then become a factor in loan contracts, for example. Previously, canonical matters could be handled through the Society but with this provision, canon law would now directly influence the actions of the university trustees. In drafting the bylaws the following month, he eliminated the reference to canon law.[25] He further noted that at Father Reinert's request, a copy of the proposed bylaws had been sent to Mr. Francis X. Gallagher, a Baltimore lawyer who defended the Catholic colleges in the 1966 *Horace Mann* case. (From various documents, both at Saint Louis and at other institutions, it is clear that Gallagher's advice was highly respected.) It may be that the criteria put forth in the *Horace Mann* case made Connelly's advice seem the best course. The canon law clause was not included when the bylaws were finally ratified. Reinert's earlier presentation in Rome regarding the canon law clause as a protection of the university's relationship to the church became moot.

The new bylaws were adopted on March 15, 1967. The change to a predominantly lay board had been achieved. The corporate purposes of the university were "the encouragement of learning and the extension of the means of education." The trustees acknowledged the rich tradition of the Jesuits at Saint Louis and stated that it would be continued:

a. The University will be publicly identified as a Catholic university and a Jesuit university;
b. The University will be motivated by the moral, spiritual, and religious inspiration and values of the Judao-Christian tradition and the Catholic Church;
c. The University will be guided by the spiritual and intellectual ideals of the Society of Jesus.[26]

These were commitments not spelled out in earlier bylaws, but with the shift to lay leadership it must have seemed important to include them.

According to the new bylaws, the university president must be a member of the Society of Jesus. The board of trustees would now have twenty-eight members, a maximum of eighteen laymen and a minimum of ten Jesuits. The bylaws state further that only five Jesuit members may come from within the university; the other Jesuit members must come from outside institutions. The board would elect its own chair from among the lay members. As noted above, the trustees chosen in 1967 were all outstanding leaders in their separate professions.

During the winter of 1966–67, as the bylaws went through several drafts, Reinert had been converted to the McGrath thesis. He now cited it as the reason why alienation should not be sought in Rome. His provincial, Linus Thro, agreed with him and together they convinced Arrupe. It should be noted that at this time the head of the American Assistancy in Rome was Rev. Harold Small, one of the participants in the coming May 1967 meeting. Another key figure who may have been helpful in getting Arrupe's approval was Rev. Vincent O'Keefe, former president of Fordham (1963–65), who was now First Councillor in Rome. O'Keefe was very well informed about American higher education and knew intimately the difficulties that Catholic colleges and universities were facing.

Reinert's adoption of the McGrath thesis concerning "ownership" led him to invite Father McGrath to make a presentation at an "Orientation Workshop" on lay trustee-ship in May 1967 at Saint Louis, which was attended by all the Jesuit presidents and a number of lawyers. The first paper discussed was that of Rev. James O'Connor, S.J., professor of canon law and moral theology of the Bellarmine School of Theology at Loyola University.[27] It made a case contrary to that presented by McGrath, but apparently was not convincing. From the list of participants at this meeting it is difficult to ascertain how many were civil lawyers and how many were canon lawyers. Whatever the extent of their disagreement, however, the outcome of the discussion favored the McGrath position. According to Reinert's summary, "There was general agreement among the civil lawyers present that according to American Law no religious order legally owned hospitals or educational institutions for which they are responsible." There was evidently agreement as to the "public trust" concept put forth by McGrath. A further argument was heard regarding tax exemption and the difficulty of borrowing money if the property were considered church property. The consensus of the group was to accept McGrath's thesis and have the Jesuit Educational Association prepare a presentation for the provincials and the Father General.[28]

Unfortunately, both Mr. Connelly, Saint Louis counsel, and Mr. Francis Gallagher, referred to above, were unable to be present at the May meeting. The lawyers in attendance included Rev. Paul Harbrecht, dean of the Law School at the University of Detroit, and Mr. Joseph G. Finnerty of Baltimore, Maryland. Others on the list, both lay and Jesuit, may well have been lawyers but they are not so identified. Charles Horgan is listed as associate trustee at Holy Cross but, as indicated earlier, was also a well-known lawyer serving as counsel to Holy Cross, Manhattanville, and the College of New Rochelle and actively involved in the *Tilton* case as advisor to Fairfield University.

The agenda of the meeting included two other important topics in addition to that of ownership of property: the implications of having a predominant presence of lay persons on a college board, and the need for separate incorporation of the Jesuit community whether or not lay persons predominated on the board. Saint Louis had completed work on its bylaws, but it had yet to complete the agreements relative to separate incorporation. Other Jesuit institutions knew that the questions involved in such action were multiple and that they would need to work out their own solutions.

It seems clear, from Father Reinert's responses to questions at this May 1967 meeting and his comments to the press and to faculty at the university, that his major goal at this time was to establish Saint Louis University within the mainstream of American higher education. In pursuing his goal, Reinert did not lack for internal critics in the Jesuit community. Some of the criticism reflected the fact that he was working with a small group of advisors—the university administrators (also trustees) and the leadership in community and province. For some Jesuits, the reconstitution of the board meant a radical loss of *their* institution, and they blamed Reinert as the doctor who performed the surgery. Despite criticism, he went on steadily from the establishment of the lay board in January 1967 to the separate incorporation of the Jesuit community, achieved on September 1, 1967, and involving a tripartite agreement among the university, the local Jesuit community, and the province.[29]

The agreement clearly states the community's support of the university: "The Jesuit Community of Saint Louis University is the agency by which the Society of Jesus makes Saint Louis University a Jesuit enterprise. It represents a commitment of the Society of Jesus' major resources— capable, professional manpower, concentrated into the service of Saint Louis University in such positions and with such quality and energy of professional effort that the University will be recognizably Jesuit in the character of its operation rather than in accidental characteristics of organization." Thus, laicization of the board was not to diminish the Jesuit character of the university.

The agreement also spells out mutual financial arrangements regarding salaries and benefits. A monthly "gift" from the community to the university should be comparable to the previous contributed services. According to the agreement, the rector of the community has no jurisdiction in the university, and with regard to university business, the president is accountable only to the board of trustees. In a codicil to the agreement it is stated that a minimum of ten Jesuits will be on the board, that the president will be a Jesuit, and that the province will make every effort to prepare and supply qualified faculty for the university.

With the signing of this agreement, Father Reinert had achieved his goal. Lines of accountability were now clear and continued support of the Jesuit mission at the university was assured. He became a resource[30] for many other presidents who wrote to him for advice and counsel as they tried to revise their governing structures. He was, of course, the main resource for his Jesuit colleagues and together with them would try to answer questions from Rome about the new arrangements.

The occasion for an explanation to Rome was a request for assistance made to Jesuit presidents by Father Edward J. Sponga, provincial of the Maryland Province, which included three Catholic universities (Saint Joseph's College in Philadelphia, Georgetown University, and Loyola College in Maryland). Father Sponga had asked permission for these schools to follow the example of Saint Louis, and in reply he had received a series of questions from Father General Arrupe. Fortunately we have a record of the questions in Arrupe's letter of November 27, 1967 and also of the answers formulated by the presidents serving on the Jesuit Educational Association commission on colleges and universities.[31] Arrupe, his council in Rome, and the American provincials who were gathered for the Thirty-first General Congregation had listened to Paul Reinert in October 1966 when he explained the reasoning behind what he was proposing, and they had approved the direction that Saint Louis was taking.

Now, a year later, Arrupe wanted specific answers to his concerns before giving further permissions.[32] Sponga's request for assistance in answering the questions gives an indication of a growing sense of unity among the presidents, soon to be translated into the formation of the Association of Jesuit Colleges and Universities. Most of them had participated in the May 1967 meeting at Saint Louis and were developing a consensus about the future of their institutions. Several presidents did not favor *predominance* of lay trustees, but all agreed to the wisdom of having some on the board. For the most part, they thought that separate incorporation of the local community was a good idea whether the board were a mixture of lay and religious or exclusively Jesuit. Some expressed a desire to involve more laymen but thought that unlike Saint Louis, they might have trouble locating the right kind of lay people. They were of the opinion, however, that even if the trustees remained exclusively Jesuit, their role had to be clarified and the lines of authority distinguished. All of them were unhappy with the interference of religious superiors in such matters as curricula, faculty hiring, speaker policies, and student discipline, and all thought that a definition of trustee powers was necessary.[33] As late as 1966, for example, the academic vice president at Saint Louis, Father Henle, had to get permission from the provincial to modify the credit requirements in philosophy and theology. Hence, the issue for the presidents was not so much a lay/religious trustee question as it was one of divesting the university of the restraints of an authority arising from religious life or based on a juridic relationship with the church.

The answers to Arrupe's questions demonstrate the strong convictions of the Jesuit presidents sitting at the table with Father Sponga. In the JEA commission meeting, the presidents pointed to the need for trustees, whether Jesuit or laymen, to be free from external dominance of any sort. The ultimate purpose of introducing laymen to the boards, they claimed, was to widen the outlook of the university by not having only Jesuit administrators act as trustees and by increasing the pool of persons with expertise in management, finance, public relations, and fund-raising. Such persons would have real authority to speak for the university to the public and "to lessen the undesirable public image of a wealthy, clergy-dominated corporation and institution." Interestingly, the enumerated reasons did not include that of recognizing the role of the laity in the church; perhaps it would have been regarded as unnecessary in the light of the declaration of the Thirty-first Congregation on that point. The presidents made it clear that a president must be accountable to the board of trustees for his duties in the university, and to his religious superior only for those personal matters unrelated to his role in the university.

Arrupe had raised the question of the "identity" of an institution as Jesuit if the responsible superiors of the Society could exercise no authority in it. Time would show this to be a question oft repeated and almost impossible to answer aside from concrete situations. The presidents pointed out that the Society had often had its name associated with apostolic causes without owning or controlling them. The crucial element was not structure but rather the extent of the commitment of the Society to a particular work as a corporate institutional activity. Assignment of personnel and resources were indicators of such commitment, but it must be supported by the creation of "an intellectual and moral environment" by the Jesuit and lay members of the university community.

In answer to the Father General's question about contractual relationships that ought to be articulated, the presidents listed eight areas: (1) the role of the Jesuit community (here the presidents made the point that it should be the local community and not the province; they feared that a contractual relationship of college or university to the province would be similar to the model of the "motherhouse" of some sisters' groups, which they claimed had not worked); (2) the role of the JEA as an agency interpreting Jesuit ideals; (3) the requirement that a Jesuit be president; (4) funds from the community should aid in fostering Jesuit aims; (5) the religious community should return "excess" funds to the university; (6) the provincial should agree to supply Jesuits for the university; (7) the university should seek out qualified Jesuits; and (8) a retirement plan should be established for Jesuits. Conditions for hiring, etc., should be the same for laymen and Jesuits. Finally, they recommended separate incorporation of the community.

In 1968, following this last recommendation from the presidents, the Fathers Provincial of the American Assistancy agreed that they should request the Father General's permission to establish separate corporations for the communities and the universities and to revise the governing structure so that laymen could be added to the boards of trustees. Paul Fitzgerald says very simply: "In practice the General accepted these proposals."[34] Each of the Jesuit universities would have to go through its own process and no two did it exactly the same way. But within the next few years almost all moved in the direction of more lay authority. Some of them kept the more restrictive form of corporate "membership" exclusively Jesuit. None of them asked permission to alienate the property or to take other actions. Most of them have required in their bylaws that the president be a Jesuit. Even when it is not a requirement in the bylaws, all but one have always chosen a Jesuit. They have continued to be very clear about their Jesuit identity and have strengthened their collaboration through the Association of Jesuit Colleges and Universities, which was set up in Washington, D.C. in 1970.

University of Notre Dame

Because of its high visibility in American higher education and its enormous Catholic following, Notre Dame's decision to transfer governing authority to a predominantly lay board was a major news event. As indicated above, Father Theodore Hesburgh and Father Paul Reinert were in frequent conversation about the need for a new form of governance for Catholic universities. They were both anxious to become places where Msgr. Ellis' vision of Catholic academic excellence would reign supreme. They were both imbued with a profound respect for the role that laymen were playing on the advisory boards of their universities and were encouraged by the growing sentiment within the church that saw lay leadership as an essential component in their future. Both of them were also deeply committed to their religious communities and the apostolate which they exercised. In addition, they were involved in national educational organizations and had serious concerns about the viability of Catholic higher education in the years ahead.[35]

It is not surprising, then, to find Father Hesburgh initiating conversations with his provincial, Father Howard Kenna, and their Superior General, Father Germain-Marie Lalande, in the summer of 1965 on the question of a new administrative arrangement for the university. The process followed at Notre Dame was different from that at Saint Louis, but both institutions reached the same goal in the spring of 1967. The University of Portland, also sponsored by the Indiana Province of Priests of Holy Cross, argued its case along with Notre Dame and made similar, although not identical, changes at the same time.

In the summer of 1965 Hesburgh was president of the International Federation of Catholic Universities and was well acquainted with Paul VI's thinking on the importance of university education under Catholic auspices. At that precise moment, the IFCU was embarking on a process to articulate the nature of a Catholic university in the light of Vatican II and its document, *The Church in the Modern World*. At a meeting in Tokyo that summer, the IFCU had proposed regional meetings to begin the preparation of a text. For the next year and a half Hesburgh would be reflecting on the importance of this question and making preparations for the Land O'Lakes meeting for the North American region of IFCU.[36] Simultaneously he was addressing the structural changes he deemed necessary for Notre Dame to become a "true university."

Encouraged by the conversations with Kenna and Lalande, Hesburgh sought out Edmund Stephan, a well-respected lawyer in Chicago and a strong member of his lay advisory board. An advisory board of lay trustees had existed at Notre Dame since 1921 which, according to the university bylaws, "shall hold, invest, and administer all endowment funds." All investments required approval by a majority of this board and, as time went on, it became a nucleus for financial decision-making. Hesburgh used the Steering Committee of this lay group as a sounding board for many of his ideas, because it was to them that grants now being received from Carnegie, Ford, etc., were entrusted. Yet the advisory board could not really make decisions about how the money would be spent or in what direction the university would go. Hesburgh found it very unsatisfactory to have to give more weight to the opinions of the religious authorities in these matters than to the lay trustees who clearly had greater expertise. He saw that they needed authority commensurate with their fund-raising and fund-managing responsibilities. In addition, he was convinced that as the role of laity was being redefined in the church, it should also be redefined in Catholic institutions.

During a visit to Stephan's home in spring of 1966, Father Hesburgh brought up the subject of restructuring the governance of the university. Over the next few months, they worked together to design a structure that would create a true partnership between lay and clerical members of a single board of trustees with full fiscal and legal responsibility. Stephan, like Schlafly at Saint Louis, was absolutely convinced that any new arrangement of governance must not weaken the Catholic character of the university or the Holy Cross influence. Under a covering letter of June 15, 1966, he submitted to Father Hesburgh a long memo on the legal aspects of what they should propose. There would be a single board of trustees with full legal and fiscal responsibility, composed of Holy Cross priests and lay persons. To assure protection of the Catholic purpose of Holy Cross's educational mission, a separate entity, the Fellows of the university, would be created. This would consist of lay/Holy Cross in equal numbers. The Fellows would have a special responsibility for the Catholic mission of the university through their role in the selection of the trustees. Furthermore, substantial changes in the university such as a merger or the sale of major pieces of property would require a two-thirds vote by the Fellows.

These preliminary suggestions were discussed at a meeting of the Development Committee of the lay advisory board with Fathers Lalande, Kenna, and Hesburgh at Land

O'Lakes on June 23–25, 1966. In a position paper offering the rationale for the transfer of governance authority, Father Hesburgh emphasized the role of the layman in the post-conciliar church, the fact that the Jesuit colleges were going through the same process, and the need to recognize the growth of Notre Dame and the resulting complexity of its operations.[37] Father Lalande underscored the need to collaborate with the lay leaders because, in his opinion, the church had been too clerical. They discussed the resistance they might find among members of the Holy Cross community and agreed that the way the proposed changes in governance were presented would be crucial. When Hesburgh raised the question of canon law and the necessity of getting permission for financial expenditure, Lalande responded that it should not be difficult to get a dispensation.

The record of this meeting demonstrates the genuine concern that marked the lay trustees' approach to the new idea: Should not Holy Cross authorities be *ex officio* trustees? Should not decisions about the sale of property require approval of the religious trustees? How will we ensure the Catholic character of the university?

Further discussion occurred at a September meeting in Rome involving Father Lalande, Father Heston (Procurator General), Fathers Kenna, Hesburgh, and Paul Waldschmidt (president of Portland), and Mr. Stephan. Following this meeting, Father Lalande wrote to Father Hesburgh that all the members of the general administration were happy to have had the opportunity to meet with him and to be informed of the plans, and that he had already presented the documents regarding the new organization to Archbishop Garrone, Secretary for the Congregation for Catholic Education, with the appropriate explanations.

A report on the Rome meeting was given to the lay board of trustees' Development Committee on November 4, 1966 by its chair, Paul Hellmuth. According to Father Hesburgh, progress was being made but some problems still needed to be solved. Among these were the issues of canon law, how to present the decision to the various publics of the university, and the relationship of Holy Cross to the university. Father Kenna pointed to the need for time to "sell" the idea to the community. He and Hesburgh were unsure about whether or not to bring the matter to the provincial chapter scheduled for the coming year. Stephan summed up the reasons for the proposed change, familiar from the Land O'Lakes meeting: (1) the increasing public character of Notre Dame resulting from its dramatic growth; and (2) the importance of involving laymen in the administration of the university both because of the Vatican II teaching and because of the expertise they could bring to an increasingly complex operation. Concern was once again expressed by the lay committee members that nothing be done to undercut the role of the Holy Cross community.

While these meetings were being held with superiors and with the lay trustees on the Development Committee, discussions on governance also formed a significant part of Holy Cross community life. On November 4, 1966, Hesburgh wrote to the Superior General, Father Lalande: "We have been having conversations with the community here regarding the new planning for the governance of the University, which we discussed in Rome. These discussions are rather difficult at times because a small, but vocal, minority want to have decisive decision over every detail. However, I believe that the majority think that the change is necessary and are mainly concerned in learning more about the totality of the plan." Hesburgh pointed out that some members wanted the matter to be sent to the provincial chapter, but "Personally, I do not believe that this would be necessary, and it might further complicate an already complicated problem."[38]

While Father Hesburgh was discussing governance in the Holy Cross community, with the advisory board of lay trustees, and also with the Notre Dame alumni board, Father Kenna was communicating his thoughts on the proposed change to members of the province. In a letter of December 13, 1966 to the entire province,[39] he presented a resume of a talk he had given to the local Notre Dame community on October 18, 1966. He identified the essential question as one of readiness to accept "laymen as partners in the government of the institution." In his opinion, the basic reason for doing so was "the preservation and increasing effectiveness of our apostolate in the universities." He quoted Andrew Greeley's comment that "the most serious obstacle to further improvement in Catholic higher education is the unsettled nature of the relationship between the school and the religious community."[40] He focused attention on the process to be followed in deciding this question, and tried to deal with possible objections. Thirty years later his arguments are clear and cogent, and one can surmise that for many members of the province they were convincing. Father Hesburgh claims that without the support of "Doc" Kenna he would never have been able to create the new board. It is important, therefore, to describe Kenna's three main arguments in some detail:

1. Notre Dame has already shared responsibility with laymen by having them serve in administration. But "it has been done on a permissive basis as a result of the free choice of the Holy Cross administrators. It

should now be done in a juridic manner so that from henceforth the laymen will have a legal right to share in the administration."

In support of this argument, Kenna cited the Danforth report *Eight Hundred Colleges Face the Future* in its identification of a *major* administrative problem in Catholic institutions as the dominant position of members of the religious order. He also referred to a recent NCEA communication citing the decision in the *Horace Mann* case and pointing to the importance of shared responsibility with laymen. He noted that current conflicts between administration and faculty or students (1965–66) were often seen as conflicts with the religious community, which was unfortunate.

2. The trend in the modern church is toward shared responsibility, as shown by Vatican II and its documents on the laity in the church and on poverty. As to the latter, Vatican II suggests that religious communities divest themselves of ownership where it is not necessary.
3. The change will benefit both the university and the congregation. Clear divisions of authority and responsibility will be achieved and laymen will have more sense of their responsibilities. Clerics on the faculty will also have more clarity as to their relationship with the university. This will reduce conflict between cleric and lay. In addition, the income for the community will be more secure if it is based on a contractual agreement.

Along with his letter, Father Kenna distributed a draft document from Mr. Stephan regarding the proposed changes. In particular, Stephan explained the reasons for the creation of the Fellows. He suggested that they be seen as analogous to shareholders in a business corporation, "delegating" a large portion of their authority to the board of trustees. Under the proposal, the approval of the Fellows would be needed for the sale or transfer of property. However, Father Kenna informed the members that in spite of this built-in protection, Father Heston was of the opinion that an indult of alienation should be requested since in canon law, the giving up of total power and responsibility on the part of Holy Cross would be "regarded in the Roman Congregation as being in the nature of alienation." Up to this point, the board of trustees had been exclusively Holy Cross, but under the proposal both the board and the Fellows would include laymen.

Kenna urged in his letter that the proposal be submitted to the provincial chapter since the chapter had the responsibility of dealing with "extraordinary" matters when it was in session. Kenna pointed out that because of the importance of Notre Dame to the order, this decision should be placed before a chapter; if the chapter approved, the proposal would then go to the Superior General.

Kenna then dealt with the major objection: transferring authority to a predominantly lay board would lead to a secularization of the university. But, he argued, even now the university is a "public trust" and "we cannot use it as we like; we must use it only for the purpose for which it has been established and the purpose for which the acquisitions of endowments and grants have been made." He thought that canon law provisions regarding property were not relevant here. But the question was, "Can we assure the university's Catholicity?" Interestingly, he quoted David Riesman and Christopher Jencks[41] on the possible secularization of Catholic colleges: "Although comparable forces [to those in Protestant-founded colleges] have been at work in Catholic education, the Catholic colleges will not necessarily become secularized either *de facto* or *de jure* as so many of the Protestant-founded ones have done and are doing. . . . Catholic higher education (like Catholicism generally) copes with the secularization by partial incorporation of it." Kenna asserted that he, of course, could not deny the danger of Notre Dame's becoming secularized, but he did not think it would happen for several reasons: (1) the continuing influence of Holy Cross by supplying competent teachers and administrators; (2) the strong influence of Catholic philosophy and theology; (3) the adoption of the Fellows model, by which Notre Dame will show real trust in the laymen; and (4) it would be unlikely that two-thirds of that group would ever de-Catholicize the university.

Father Kenna's conclusion was an inspiring one: "This is not primarily a Holy Cross institution; it is a Catholic institution which Holy Cross has been privileged to found, to build, and to cement through its labor, its sacrifices and, indeed, its heart's blood, but it has been done for the Church and for God and his people. . . . Holy Cross has traditionally been open; it has traditionally been ready to go along with the changes which seem to make more effective its apostolate. I think this one is now necessary."

The strength of this support from the provincial, Father Kenna, and the ready agreement of the Superior General certainly lightened the burden of proof which lay on Father Hesburgh. His own arguments for establishing a primarily lay board of trustees were given in a paper he delivered to the provincial chapter on January 25, 1967. On the previous day Father Waldschmidt, president of the University of Portland, had placed his proposed new governmental structure before the chapter.

Father Hesburgh had already explained Notre Dame's position in a letter to the wide "Notre Dame family" which he had issued on January 18, 1967, because of pressure from the media in the wake of the Webster College decision. Now, in his presentation to the chapter,[42] Hesburgh reviewed his discussions with Kenna and Lalande for the past year and his own initial reluctance to change the governance. He had three reasons for not wanting to change: the preservation of the Catholicity of Notre Dame; the preservation of the role of the community in the university; and the difficulty of working out the financial relationships between the university and the community. He acknowledged that he had received great assistance in his thinking from Father Waldschmidt and the Portland plan, and said that Notre Dame "has fairly well adopted that plan in toto" (although a closer examination shows many differences).

Hesburgh described his meetings with the lay trustees over the past year and noted the fact that lay and clerical administration and trustees attended the Land O'Lakes meeting with Fathers Kenna and Lalande. Father Lalande was "way out ahead of the rest of us," and had urged further conversation with alumni, benefactors, and trustees. Hesburgh reported his own discussions of the plan with some key figures in government and foundations. He couched the urgency to act on this proposal in terms of competition with other universities for fellowships, funds, and various programs where it was often hard to explain who runs the university without "fudging" it. Another source of pressure were the faculty, who were organizing and who wanted a role in decision-making. Questions of tenure and academic freedom required a balance of clerical and lay members in the total governance. Hesburgh cited the "Statement on the Governance of Colleges and Universities" by AAUP, AGB, and ACE (American Council on Education) and the conflict on academic freedom at St. John's, which had cast such a shadow on Catholic higher education, as further reasons for moving toward greater lay involvement in university governance. Finally, he argued, the whole climate of post-Vatican II mandated a change to lay participation.

Hesburgh's speech sheds light on the "network" of presidents. He had spoken just "on Thursday" with Paul Reinert, who was feeling pressure because of the Webster College announcement and was going forward with his own news release of January 21. He was aware that many other colleges were considering similar changes and thought Notre Dame should be out front. The financial pressure was vividly portrayed by his allusion to the fact that Notre Dame's budget was now forty times that of the total province budget. He noted that the process for investments was archaic in that it required local, provincial, and general approval. Reinert had told him that such operations would be left out of canon law when the new Code was promulgated, but Notre Dame needed to act now since there was a big need for money. In fact, he saw the need to raise fifty million dollars for the university in the next five years, and this would require dedicated trustees. There was also some fear that the federal government would adopt a law denying funds to church-related universities, and unfortunately, Hesburgh observed, total control by clerics was perceived as "church" control. He reflected on the benefit that had come from separating the roles of superior and president in 1958, and indicated he was now seeking something of the same clarity in regard to the role of the community vis-à-vis the university, a role currently enhanced by the competence and professionalism of Holy Cross faculty.

In presenting the legal plan drawn up with Mr. Stephan, Hesburgh likened it to that of Harvard; the Board of Fellows would be similar to Harvard's Board of Overseers. There would be no need to change the original charter. Residual power would lie with the Fellows at Notre Dame. Rome had already given approval, and the local bishop was favorable. Most of the local council approved. Despite his earlier reluctance to go in this direction, Father Hesburgh stated he was now convinced that the proposed structure would safeguard the Catholicity of the university and provide for the continuation of the role of Holy Cross. The addition of outstanding persons as trustees would allow the possibility of creating a *great* Catholic university. To meet this goal all kinds of resources were needed: administrative, financial, and educational talent. Hesburgh was convinced that lay trustees would be successful in acquiring them.

Hesburgh's position paper highlights the causes for the change in governance at the University of Notre Dame. While it makes some reference to the Vatican II theology of the laity, it is clear that the pressure of size and the need to amass resources to support a "new" Notre Dame gave urgency to the task of transformation. The recognition of the "emerging" layman was a timely support for what needed to be done, but had there been no Vatican II it is probable that Hesburgh would still have argued for a change in governance.

Further elucidation of Hesburgh's reasons can be found in a speech given by Rev. John Walsh, C.S.C. (the academic vice president at Notre Dame) at the 1968 IFCU Assembly in Kinshasa. As background for discussion of the text of *The Catholic University in the Modern World,* Father Walsh thought it would be helpful for the delegates to know about the changes being made in the United States and particularly at Notre Dame.[43] In explaining the composition of the new board and the Fellows, he argued: "When the members of a religious order constitute exclusively the Board of

Trustees of a university, they can hardly help letting their decisions as board members be colored by considerations of the good of the order. . . . In addition, because these trustees are members of religious orders, the institutional Church has the power to control them through their vows and through Canon Law. There is not the necessary freedom from ecclesiastical control, as there must be from any outside force, to enable the university to be autonomous and act independently as a university. . . . The influence of the Church will come through the convictions and dedication of the university administration, faculty, students, alumni, and friends who do, in fact, control the university. . . . There would appear to be no cause for fear that the religious presence in a university will be diluted by sharing of ownership and governance with the laity."

The lack of direct oversight by the religious community or church authorities might also strengthen ecumenical endeavors. Father Walsh cited the situation of Catholic universities in Canada, where church-related colleges existed within and dependent on provincial universities, as one viable alternative. While no institution in the United States had actually merged with a secular university, he pointed to the recent move of Woodstock College to create a joint program with Union Theological Seminary at Columbia University as another alternative. Finally, he focused on the question of academic freedom and the importance of the question in the United States, where standards have been adopted which safeguard the professor's freedom to teach. Hence, it was necessary to make clear that decisions regarding faculty are within the realm of faculty competence, subject only to review by the board of trustees.

Arguments such as these by Father Walsh in 1968 reflect the prevailing spirit within the chapter at Notre Dame in January 1967. There were some opposing opinions expressed by chapter delegates, most of which dealt with the loss of control of the university by the Congregation of Holy Cross and questioned the need for making this change. But the final vote was thirty-eight to four in favor of the Notre Dame plan (and forty-one to one in favor of the Portland plan). By March 25, 1967 an indult of alienation had been received from Rome and the decrees of the chapter had been approved. The Vice Superior General, Rev. Bernard Mullahy, had already written to Father Kenna on May 27, 1966 that Hesburgh's plan for Notre Dame "seems to me to provide more definite guarantees for the preservation of the interests of the Church than any other formula which I have heard proposed."[44] From the beginning, Father Lalande had favored the change as part of the post-Vatican II spirit, which he interpreted to mean more commitment to the apostolic mission of the community and less to a particular institution.

Strong support had also come from Pope Paul VI. In a letter of January 27, 1964 to Father Hesburgh, Father Lalande had reported on a visit with the pope at which he had spoken about Hesburgh's role in the IFCU. In addition to his comments on Hesburgh's leadership in IFCU, Pope Paul had pointed out that institutions could no longer be run the way they had been. "He holds that we must entrust laymen with genuine responsibilities and that we must endeavor to find new structures that will enable us to entrust our laity with real responsibilities for the carrying out of which (and these are his very words) 'they are more competent than we are.'"[45] Father Lalande assured Father Hesburgh that he could count on the Holy Father's esteem and trust.

At a special meeting of the board of trustees on March 28, 1967, under the chairmanship of Father Kenna, the decision was made. The trustees present, in addition to

Fathers Kenna and Hesburgh, were: Rev. Edmund P. Joyce, Rev. John Cavanaugh, Rev. Charles I. McCarragher, and Rev. John E. Walsh. They now voted to reorganize the governing board of the university. The plan had already been widely discussed and, in addition to the approval of the chapter, it had been approved by the General Council and by authorities at the Vatican. The trustees now accepted "in principle" the plan drawn up by Father Joyce for the financial arrangements to be made with Holy Cross. The structures of Fellows, half lay and half Holy Cross, and of a predominantly lay board of trustees were approved and the former bylaws were repealed. The reasons cited were: (1) the increasing public character of the university with consequent financial support from foundations, corporations, and the public at large; (2) the dramatic growth in the past few decades leading to unprecedented and complex problems of administration; (3) the need to draw on all available skills; and (4) the importance of granting the laity a more independent and responsible role in governance.

The trustees then adopted the new Statutes of the University and elected the non-*ex officio* Fellows: Robert Galvin, Paul Hellmuth, Rev. John J. Cavanaugh, C.S.C., I. A. O'Shaughnessy, J. Peter Grace, Rev. Charles I. McCarragher, C.S.C., Edmund A. Stephan, and Bernard J. Voll. The *ex officio* Fellows were the provincial superior of Indiana Province, the religious superior of the Holy Cross community at Notre Dame, the president, provost, and executive vice president of the university, and the chair of the board of trustees. The Fellows would also become members of the board of trustees; there would be thirty to sixty trustees, with a majority of laymen. The president of Notre Dame would be elected from the Congregation of Holy Cross, Indiana Province.

In the many presentations that Hesburgh made regarding the new structure of university leadership to faculty, trustees, students, and his fellow Holy Cross brothers, he spoke with deep conviction about the distinctive mission he envisioned for Notre Dame as a great Catholic University. He explicated his vision in a somewhat more poetic letter than he usually wrote to the faculty, describing the ideal Notre Dame as "a beacon, shining with the great light of intelligence illumined by faith, a bridge across the chasm of misunderstandings that divide rich and poor, believers and unbelievers, and a crossroads where all the vital intellectual currents of our times meet in dialogue, where the church confronts the modern world with all its insights and all its anguishes."[46]

By arguing for a change in governance which would eliminate clerical control of the university, Father Hesburgh was not proposing that Notre Dame become a secular university. Although he recognized Sister Jacqueline Grennan's courage, he had a different vision for Notre Dame. Like Paul Reinert, Ann Ida Gannon, and many other presidents, he desired a partnership with the laity, not an abandonment by the religious community, and a strengthened Catholic university at the service of the church and society, not an institution devoid of a faith tradition and a living faith community. The decision to move to a predominantly lay board in 1967 would color the subsequent history of Notre Dame in a way that led to a partial fulfillment of Hesburgh's vision.

Mundelein College

A very different process of changing the membership of the board of trustees was underway at Mundelein College in Chicago.[47] Incorporated on January 16, 1930, Mundelein was governed by the religious community of the Sisters of Charity of the Blessed Virgin Mary. The faculty in the 1960s was about two-thirds sisters and one-third lay; there were eighty-three full-time and part-time faculty in 1967, including thirty-one full-time lay faculty. Two of the vice presidents were lay men as well as an assistant dean, registrar, director of public relations, and director of financial aid. In 1966 the president, Sister Ann Ida Gannon, was intent on adding more lay men to the faculty and at the same time began planning for a lay board of trustees. She was a woman of vision and action, a "first" among sisters to be elected to the boards of higher education associations in Washington. She was strongly affected by the spirit of Vatican Council II and the challenge issued by Msgr. Ellis to the Catholic colleges. Her goal was not that of Reinert or Hesburgh—to create a "great" Catholic university—but rather to develop a women's college in the Chicago area that would be known for a strong liberal arts program led by a first-rate faculty.

At Mundelein the decisions regarding the religious congregation and the college were so intertwined that Sister Ann Ida recalled having been canonically appointed superior of the community in 1957 but never legally elected president, a position she assumed at the same time. It was only when she began the process of seeking a federal loan for a dormitory that she discovered the underlying confusion that existed between the canonical "council" and the legal "board of trustees." Bylaws enacted at her behest in 1960 clarified some of the areas of decision-making and, for the first time, established legal records of board activities distinct from General Council records.

In 1966 the Catholic colleges in Chicago had experienced an episcopal attempt to control their decisions, and had organized under the leadership of local AAUP chapters to resist a decree of Cardinal Cody which mandated prior permission for any priests who might be invited into the diocese to teach or lecture. Ann Ida strongly supported those on her faculty who served on the AAUP committee, and although the incident was settled without public confrontation, the experience left her with new insights about the importance of maintaining proper independence of local church authority.

Between 1960 and 1966 Sister Ann Ida examined governance questions from many points of view. As a philosopher she was deeply interested in the whole question of women's education. As a religious, she was aware of the apostolic desires of her sisters and the role that the college played in their vocation. Contrary to the solution embraced by Webster College, she thought that her experience with lay administrators and advisory trustees suggested another way of securing the future of Mundelein. In an announcement made at the time, she spoke of the obligation of a Catholic college in the post-conciliar era to prepare its students "not only to build a bridge to the contemporary world but to cross that bridge and to ensure that the decrees, *especially as they refer to the laity* [emphasis mine] will be realized in their lives.[48]

Since the current Superior General agreed with Sister Ann Ida's own perception of the future role of the laity in the church, she decided to move on the governance issue while this superior was still in office. Before asking the religious trustees to share the governing authority with a new board of trustees including lay people, she discussed the plan with the entire faculty. Sister Ann Ida initiated a discussion about lay membership on the board at a faculty meeting of February 7, 1967. In the course of answering questions, she explained the background for her proposal.

Under Illinois law, the corporation of the religious congregation owned the college but the responsibilities of college and community were anything but clear. She showed herself thoroughly conversant with the discussions going on elsewhere and identified several of the questions which resulted from arrangements like those currently in place at Mundelein: for example, Were canonical permisssions needed for borrowing by academic institutions? Who owned properties received from donors by the college over the years since its founding? What about the contributed salaries of the sisters (in the previous year at Mundelein these were valued at $500,000)? In the light of these issues, what should be done? Her own opinion rested on the McGrath thesis; in response to a question regarding the 1966 *Horace Mann* case, she said that Mundelein could be described as "an institution owned and operated by Catholics but it is not a Catholic Institution if that term were to mean owned or directly supervised by the diocesan or church authorities."[49]

Interestingly, Sister Ann Ida linked the proposal for a lay board to a recommendation made in 1957 by Msgr. Ellis and Lewis Mayhew, after a visit to the Mundelein campus, that *all* the faculty should be more involved in the planning and implementation of the college program. The resulting success in including lay faculty within the administration now led to a consideration of adding lay persons to the board.

The president's proposal was for a gradual change in the composition of the board rather than a more immediate and radical change. In a letter to the Sisters of Charity in August 1967, Ann Ida explained the proposed structure. A new board of trustees would be created of six sisters and ten laymen who would assume legal control of the college. However, ownership of the property would continue to be vested in the Members of the corporation. These Members would include the Superior General, her councillors, the secretary and treasurer general and the president, plus five more sisters who would be elected annually by the Mundelein community. The Members would have decisive vote on such important matters as selling the property, dissolving the corporation, changing the articles of incorporation, or changing the nature of the college. Hence, the community would still have ultimate control. But in subsequent discussion the sisters proposed that lay trustees be included in the corporation. The makeup of the corporation was then modified and the corporation defined its members as: five sisters designated by the sisters on the college faculty (to be elected formally by the board); three lay trustees; three members of the board of directors of the congregation (president, one vice president, and treasurer); and the president of the college.

With this change, the new bylaws were approved by the existing board of trustees on August 16, 1967. Ten lay trustees were then elected. The function of the board, according to the public announcement, was "to select, counsel with and support the president of the College, to promote understanding and cooperation between society and the college by interpreting the opinions and judgments of each of these to the others; to understand and approve the kind of education offered by the college, ascertain that its quality meets the highest standards possible, and assist in the planning for educational growth; to assure that the college fulfills the distinctive purposes for which it was established, and to oversee the acquisition and investment of funds and the management of facilities for the implementation of the educational program." The bylaws also stipulated that members of the faculty would sit on the committees of the board and would have a vote. This was a unique provision among the institutional bylaws studied by the author.

Various religious traditions were represented among the new trustees, giving testimony to the spirit of ecumenism which Ann Ida felt was important. In her announcement of the new trustees, she said: "Basic to all of the changes is the effort to implement the directives of Vatican Council II which called for increased dialog among all men who are seeking to serve society and further the brotherhood of men."[50] At the first meeting of the new board, Mr. Lee Schooler, a member of the Jewish community, was elected chair. According to the *Mundelein College Report* of October/November 1967, it was the first time that a non-Catholic had been elected chair of a legal board of trustees of a Catholic college or university.

Before the new board of fourteen members could begin functioning, some ambiguities regarding the mutual responsibilities of corporation Members and trustees had to be resolved. At a meeting of the Members on December 27, 1967, it was agreed that there was no intention of setting up two policy-making boards. Corporate Members could not initiate policy or elect trustees. Their chief purpose was to approve or veto trustee decisions "insofar as this is provided in the bylaws."[51] While an inference could be made from the composition of the Members that the president of the college would necessarily be a Sister of Charity, this was not stated explicitly.

A special feature of the bylaws at Mundelein was the provision that five Members would be selected by and from the sisters on the faculty. Ann Ida described the plan as one that took into account the special investment of the sisters in the work of the college. I have not come upon any other

Catholic college that followed this same line of thought. As a matter of fact, over the next two decades, under the strong recommendations of the Association of Governing Boards and accrediting agencies, most institutions denied membership on boards to faculty members, arguing that since faculty can appeal to the board it would be a conflict of interest to serve on the board. But in 1967 this opinion had not yet been widely adopted, and the identity of sisters as faculty and sisters as members of the religious community that had founded the college made such conflict of interest seem to be a straw man or a legal fiction. It was hard for sisters to think that the interests of college and community would contradict one another, and so for the moment it seemed a good way to keep the sisters involved in the work of the college at the board level as well as on the faculty. It also meant that the mission of the Sisters of Charity of the Blessed Virgin Mary would have the opportunity to pass on the tradition of their congregation to the new trustees.

Unlike Webster, Notre Dame, or Saint Louis, Mundelein never even considered the possibility of seeking a canonical indult to alienate the property. Control over the property was retained in the corporation, a majority of whose Members were sisters, and there was no transfer of assets to a lay group. After the "Cardinal Cody affair" of 1966, Sister Ann Ida had no desire to enter into a discussion of Mundelein's plans with the archbishop of Chicago, and she had no Mother General in Rome with connections to the Vatican who might have raised the issue. Her own thinking had been strongly influenced by the theory of John McGrath; however in this instance his argument was not really necessary because the ownership was still vested in the Members of the corporation, a two-thirds majority of whom were from the congregation.

Like her colleagues, Fathers Hesburgh and Reinert, Ann Ida Gannon remained in office long enough to oversee the transition to a more mature lay partnership at Mundelein. In her statements at the time of the 1967 decision, she gave clear voice to her motives for action: the Ellis challenge to achieve greater academic excellence, the changing nature of the faculty and administration, the many new movements in American higher education and in religious life, and above all, her personal commitment to the ideals of Vatican Council II.

In the case of Mundelein there was no immediate financial pressure comparable to that being experienced by the large universities seeking to develop expensive research capacity, nor was there the need to meet governmental criteria for institutional grants similar to that of the New York State colleges. It simply seemed to be the right thing to do if Mundelein hoped to find lay support for its efforts to update its educational programs and to continue its Christian mission. And it seemed important to Sister Ann Ida to seize the moment and act courageously. This she did.

University of Portland

On January 24, 1967, only a day before Father Hesburgh spoke to the Congregation of Holy Cross chapter, the president of the University of Portland, Rev. Paul Waldschmidt, briefed the chapter members on the reasons why Portland wanted an independent governing board.[52] He reviewed the difficult financial picture of the university and reminded the chapter that in 1958, when Father Kenna was both superior and president of Portland, there had been serious consideration of discontinuing the university. Unlike Notre Dame, Portland had no state charter since Oregon did not

charter educational institutions at the time of its foundation; universities and colleges were simply private corporations. Portland, according to its articles of incorporation,
was underwritten by the Congregation of Holy Cross, Indiana Province, and "implicitly" by the University of Notre
Dame—not a healthy situation, according to Waldschmidt.
Consequently, after the chapter of 1961 the university
leaders had worked hard to develop a lay board of trustees
with purely advisory status. Now, he was proposing that
they find a way "of getting individuals of significant influence interested sufficiently in the University to assist in the
development of funds to meet its needs."

In 1965 Waldschmidt had proposed the idea of a genuine
board of trustees; his preliminary conversations with some
of the advisory lay trustees had made it clear that they were
tired of membership on various Catholic boards where decision-making power was still in the hands of the bishop
or religious community. Said Waldschmidt: "They were
also aware of the traditional Catholic procedure where
Father asks the Board for their opinion and then does as he
pleases." Since he had talked with them about a genuine
board of trustees, a jump in fund-raising had occurred. But
a problem remained in that persons in Oregon thought that
if Portland was in financial trouble, "Notre Dame will bail
you out." Waldschmidt thought that this perception hin-
dered serious fund-raising. A real board of trustees would
also give visible continuity to an institution that had been
plagued with changes of administration and programs.

Waldschmidt noted a certain complacency among young
C.S.C.'s who saw the provincial as the one who decided
whether or not they remained on the faculty. Since there
were some ongoing discussions about creating a West-
ern Province, that was another reason to develop Portland

separately from Notre Dame. Interestingly, Waldschmidt expressed concern for a growing secularization at the university under the present governance and argued that there was a need to "focus" the attention of everyone at the university on the Christian purpose of their work and to avoid an attitude of leaving it to Holy Cross. He pointed out that Portland was different from Notre Dame; it was urban, co-educational, and had a less formal atmosphere and a more liberal reputation. The increasing need for laymen in administration was causing the university to raise questions about the overall governance.

Waldschmidt saw the solution to Portland's need in a "strong governing body to which the president and other key officers can turn." He proposed a change in the financial arrangements so that the provincial chapter would decide how much to contribute to the university rather than decide how much the university should pay the province. He also proposed that the provincial and council no longer approve the annual budget, and he urged an end to the need for approval of borrowing and/or indebtedness by the provincial and/or the Superior General and Holy See. Nor should building plans, investments, and divesting of property need such approval. In his opinion, all of these permissions were clouded in ambiguity and as a result, very often no permission was asked.

Waldschmidt further proposed that the governing board appoint the president, vice presidents, secretary, and treasurer of the university. The Priests of Holy Cross of Indiana Province, Inc. would still be Portland's legal owner (insofar as a non-profit corporation has owners), but the actual owner would be the board of trustees (called Board of Regents) who would have authority to use the assets and operate the institution. The university currently was considered an extension of a religious house (according to canon law); it would now become a secular corporation.

Waldschmidt proposed that there should be five members of Holy Cross on a forty-member Board of Regents. The relationship between the university and Holy Cross would be contained in a Deed and Trust Agreement which would safeguard the Catholic identity of the institution and give Holy Cross the prior and exclusive rights to provide services to the Roman Catholic students while also providing support for other Christian and non-Christian religious services. (There was a large non-Catholic student population at Portland.)

The proposed agreement contained a reversionary clause in favor of Holy Cross in case the assets should cease to be used for the purposes now agreed to. A process for arbitration was outlined in the instance of a disagreement as to any alleged "breach of trust." The agreement also prohibited the sale or transfer of the property without approval of Holy Cross. A further agreement between Holy Cross and the Regents assured the latter of continued support from the province.

Waldschmidt's address to the chapter reflected his correspondence during the preceding year with Father Lalande. He had shared the Superior General's views with Father Kenna in June 1966.[53] Father Lalande, he reported, had advised referring in the agreement to the "Provincial of the Province within which the university is located" rather than to the Provincial of Indiana Province, since a change might be made in the designation of a new province for the West. He also did not favor having the provincial on the board or a specific number of Holy Cross priests. Lalande also did not wish the Superior General to have the responsibility of serving on an arbitration committee or appointing the members of it, as was proposed. He expressed the opinion that people making the appointments should be in the United States and familiar with the kind of Catholic education that exists here. Hence, when Waldschmidt made his presentation to the chapter, he knew it would probably be approved in Rome. The chapter vote confirmed him in his plan.

The new Board of Regents was set up and the Deed and Trust Agreement became effective April 20, 1967. Once again, we find a different model of governance from the others we have examined, but it contained the same fundamental decision to separate religious authority from academic responsibility. Portland did not include the provincial, *ex officio,* on the board, simply specifying five Holy Cross priests.

It is interesting to note, moreover, that even where the same province was the sponsor of two universities and the same provincial chapter considered the requests of the two presidents, the solutions were different. Unlike Notre Dame with its Fellows (half lay and half religious), Portland created a lay board but retained the ultimate control over the assets in case of dissolution in the Holy Cross Congregation. Fortunately, these provisions have not been tested in either case.

Saint Michael's College

Saint Michael's College presents an altogether different situation.[54] The president, Rev. Gerald Dupont, S.S.E., was widely respected among his colleagues in Catholic higher education and was known for his support of the move to new governance structures.[55] However, at home he had problems with some of his brother Edmundites and with the Superior General, Very Reverend Eymard P. Galligan. At Saint Michael's the transition to an independent board was begun at the same time as Notre Dame and Saint Louis but ran into problems resulting from internal administrative dissatisfaction and a clash between the president and the Superior General. The "laicization" process was not completed until 1994 when the board began to elect its own chair.

In April 1966 Dupont submitted a proposal to the existing board of trustees, exclusively members of the Society of St. Edmund, for a reorganization of the governance structure. Two years earlier, the newly-elected Superior General had expressed the desire not to be on the board until a reorganization had been effected. He wanted the entire General Council and/or the General Curia of the Society as well as the Superior General to be *ex officio* board members. Dupont agreed with this suggestion, provided that at the same time laymen be added to the board. He agreed to have the entire council as *ex officio* trustees but pointed out that under the present number of trustees allowed (eight), he could not invite the entire council until the terms of three other Edmundites expired on July 1, 1966. At that time, they would seek permission to enlarge the board to fifteen trustees. He proposed that they add to the eight Edmundites (five *ex officio* and two others, as well as the president) two members of the diocesan clergy and five laymen. The eight-to-seven ratio thus constructed would keep control of the college in the hands of the Society; in this, he followed the ideas of Stanford.

After describing earlier attempts to revise the bylaws in such a way as to reconcile them with the constitution of the Society (one in a 1953 proposal and another in 1964), Dupont proposed increasing the membership to seventeen, thus giving opportunity for six lay members. He also proposed that the board elect its own chair, thus moving away from the Superior General as *ex officio* chair. In the two earlier attempts at amendment, the trustees were unable to take action because they could not clarify the relationship between the college and the community. The same crucial issue surfaced as soon as Dupont's proposal was on the table.

The proposed new bylaws stated that "The property, affairs, business and concerns of the College shall be vested in the Board of Trustees," following both McGrath and Stanford. However Dupont, citing Stanford on this point, also made it clear that the ecclesiastical nature of the properties was recognized and must be safeguarded. After speaking of the legal control of the trustees and their accountability to civil authority in virtue of their charter, he stated: "These same acts of the college, namely the borrowing of money, the purchase of real estate, the sale of land, and the like, have no ecclesiastical validity without the approval of the religious board of control and sometimes of a higher religious authority."[56] Dupont's comment is revealing as to his own conservative disposition: "It is clear that the board of trustees of a college run by a religious community cannot be the sole and final arbiter of college affairs, as is the case for secular colleges." But how would such ecclesiastical control be exercised? The membership of the board would be the key to the retention of "control" by the Society and its mediation of ecclesiastical authority.

Another interesting point in the proposed bylaws is that the board "will approve the choice of the President made by the Superior General." What we are dealing with here is obviously what came to be called a "two-tier" kind of trustee authority, with the council of the religious community able to continue making the significant decisions about property and presidential leadership while turning over the jurisdiction for policies, programs, and finances of the college to the board. Dupont was anything but revolutionary.

On October 24, 1966 the board voted to expand its membership to a maximum of twenty-four. Permission was requested from the State of Vermont and granted in November. The new bylaws were then approved on December 16, 1966, and the first meeting of the expanded board was held January 21, 1967. While this was actually the same day on which Paul Reinert announced the creation of a new board at Saint Louis University, the change in the board structure at Saint Michael's was far less complete. Confusion about the roles of the college administration and the Edmundite General Council delayed the actual functioning of the board for almost a year, since its authority under the bylaws was not clear. At its meeting on May 31, 1968, the chair of the board, Father Galligan, said that the Edmundite General Chapter would be meeting in July and it would consider the relationship of the two entities; in his opinion this would assist in further revision of the bylaws of the board.

Meanwhile, Dupont had received recommendations from Earl McGrath regarding the administrative structure and functioning of the college. It is obvious that the officers of the administration were not as professionally inclined as Dupont wished. He complained about them in a letter to Galligan and was obviously not happy with his own lack of authority over them. The board members during 1967 and 1968 were increasingly distressed by the kind of financial reporting given to them, and board minutes indicate tension between Dupont and the finance officer. The presence of the General Council on the board did not seem to be working well because of its dual relationship to the president.

Things came to a head in the summer of 1968 when the Superior General, Father Galligan, all but demanded Dupont's resignation as president. From June 3 on there were conversations and written communications about the reasons for this request.[57] Dupont explained that under the new bylaws only the board could ask for his resignation. He questioned the authority of the General Council to do so. The Superior General responded that he was quite willing to go through the board but he had hoped to spare Dupont the humiliation of being asked to resign. There is nothing to suggest that the development of the new lay board caused the action of the Superior General, especially since Dupont had built in all the safeguards of control for the Society. Was there internal objection to the extension of the board to laymen? Were the new lay trustees unwilling to accept the controls? Did the General Council vote as a block? In the year and a half between the adoption of the 1966 bylaws and the summer of 1968, what had happened? The answer is not clear.

Although the local press at the time of Father Dupont's eventual resignation claimed that he was opposed by "conservative" elements in the community, the problem seems to have been more a personal conflict between the president and the Superior General over Dupont's style of leadership. According to Galligan, in his letter of August 29, his "one fear about the Board is that we will lose our good lay trustees for want of any function to perform. They are talented, capable, and willing to be of service but I cannot help but feel that we are not responding to their talents, their capabilities, and their desires to serve."[58] He denied that he was circumventing the board or unduly controlling its actions. Rather, he gave as his reason for seeking Dupont's resignation the fact that the college needed fresh, new, alive approaches; he thought Dupont did not recognize the signs of the times and lacked ability to communicate, to delegate, and to respect subsidiarity. These last observations suggest the fundamental problem that some members of the community had with Dupont; those who knew him recall today that they considered him a forceful leader but one who did not respect the ideas of others.

Galligan informed Dupont in the same letter that he would recommend to the board that it ask for Dupont's resignation and that he was willing to abide by the board's decision. The board's next meeting was scheduled for September 27–28. There is no evidence of a response to this from Dupont nor any indication that he took any action. Possibly he wanted to complete work on a "Statement on the Relationship of the Society of St. Edmund to St. Michael's College," which was very important to him and which he presumably presented to the board. It was based on the poll of members taken by a committee set up by the General Chapter. The final draft is dated September 1, 1968 but was not adopted by the Society and the board until September 11, 1970.[59]

On September 6, twenty days before the scheduled board meeting, Father Dupont submitted his resignation to Galligan[60] in a very concise note asking Galligan to so inform the trustees. On September 12, 1968, Galligan issued a public statement concerning Dupont's resignation, expressing gratitude for his leadership, and explaining that at the board meeting of September 27–28 an advisory committee would be set up to assist in the selection of his successor. The announcement concluded in a most surprising way: "Father Dupont has been requested and has agreed to remain as Acting President until his successor is chosen."[61]

A reading of the minutes for 1968–69 reveals the tension in the board meetings with Dupont as acting president and the board interviewing candidates for his job. A great deal of time was devoted to budget matters and to the financial arrangements that needed to be considered between the college and the Society of St. Edmund as they continued to work out the statement regarding their relationship, which had been drafted by Dupont in the summer of 1968.

Saint Michael's may well be an example of the numerous colleges that struggled to keep control in the hands of the religious authorities while striving at the same time to adopt a mode of governance that could be considered "independent." The nature of the board structure was modified, not radically changed, and an agreement was hammered out that would express a new relationship between the college and its founding group but would not surrender ultimate control.

Father Dupont died in 1974 and the board minutes are singularly silent about the event. The board accepted a gift from Michael and Margaret McCarthy (he a trustee) and honored their request to erect a memorial on the campus in Dupont's honor. Newspaper accounts, as at the time of his resignation, again linked his forced resignation to opposition from conservative Edmundites, presumably because of his initiative regarding the board. But as we have seen, nothing in the record suggests that was the basis for their complaint. Dupont, after all, had kept the control in the hands of the S.S.E. General Council and even after his forced resignation in 1968, he accepted membership on the board and served as a trustee from 1972 to 1974.

In the meantime, the search for Dupont's successor resulted, ironically, in the choice of Saint Michael's first lay president. Since the bylaws gave the board only the power to ratify the choice of the Superior General, one must conclude that Father Galligan and his council were sympathetic to the inclusion of more laity in the college administration. Mr. Bernard Boutin, a trustee, was elected president in 1969 and served until 1974. When he resigned, Rev. Francis Moriarty, S.S.E., agreed to serve as interim president, but he declined the permanent office. On April 2, 1976, Edward Henry became president and the line of lay presidents has continued. However, the separation of the board's authority from that of the religious community, in this case the Society of St. Edmund, was less clear-cut than at any of the other colleges studied here, and was only finalized in 1994.

Fordham University

In earlier discussion we have referred to the meeting held by Paul Reinert at Saint Louis University in May 1967 to "orientate" the other Jesuit presidents toward lay trusteeship and shared governance. One of the attendees was Rev. Leo McLaughlin, S.J., president of Fordham University, and he returned home enthusiastic about the meeting. He gave a report at the June meeting of the Jesuit presidents on the subject of lay boards that was consonant with Reinert's actions at Saint Louis University. However, Fordham's path to a lay board would be a more difficult one, partly because of its history and partly because it was in New York State.[62]

When the Jesuits assumed responsibility in 1842 from the bishop of New York for what at that time was "St. John's College," a lay board of trustees already existed. However, this was soon changed to one composed exclusively of

Jesuits. In 1916 the rector, Father Joseph Mulry, informed the provincial that Cardinal Farley wanted lay trustees and would not approve plans for a $500,000 campaign for the college until lay trustees were appointed. Mulry saw this as a move to gain control of Fordham and stated that, in his opinion, it would be contrary to Jesuit rules. In November 1927 a new rector, Father McCloskey, drew up a plan for a board of trustees with eight non-Jesuit and seven Jesuit members, with Cardinal Farley as chair having veto power in regard to finances and the appointment and removal of rectors. The names of the non-Jesuit trustees to be included were: Msgr. Lavelle, Bishop Hayes, Morgan J. O'Brien, Bourke Cockran, John Whalen, and perhaps John D. Cummins, certainly a distinguished group of lay and clerical leaders in the archdiocese. Before the plan could be implemented, however, a new rector was appointed and the whole idea was dropped.

At that time the title *rector* included both the office of superior of the community and president of the university. As a result, the administrative structure of the university was tightly linked to the religious community. Since canon law prescribed a six-year term for the superior (or rector, when that term was used), the president was also changed every six years. Several experiments in changing the roles were carried on at Fordham as in some other Jesuit institutions: president-rector with the superior of the community accountable to the rector; superior-rector with the president accountable to the superior; and so on. Finally in 1967 a distinct and clear separation was made between the two offices when Rev. Leo McLaughlin was appointed president and Rev. James Hennessey was named rector, i.e., superior, of the Jesuit community.

Up to this point, there had been little formality about the university board of trustees, its bylaws and its responsibilities. Community officials made decisions about property and even curriculum and honorary degrees were approved by the provincial. The need for a group that would advise and assist him had led President-Rector Laurence McGinley,[63] president from 1949 to 1963, to establish a board of lay trustees on May 22, 1959. In announcing this new board, Father McGinley made it clear, however, that "the legal ownership of Fordham and ultimate policy control will continue to reside in the Society of Jesus." For the time being, the legal trustees continued to be all Jesuits, but there were some joint meetings in 1964 at which the lay board chair presided. By October 1967, the list of trustee committees included both advisory and legal trustees, and both Jesuits and non-Jesuits.

The self-study done at Fordham in preparation for the Middle States accreditation visit in 1963 stated that "Under civil law the authority of the university resides in, and its properties are held by, the Board of Trustees." It also stated that *all* administrative authority is held by the president and rector (McGinley) appointed by the Superior General and for legal purposes elected by the board.

In reviewing Fordham's self-study and in its own report of March 1963, Middle States called attention to fundamental questions of mission and administration which must be addressed. In all, it said, the "image" of Fordham was very unclear. Was it a seminary, a graduate school, an undergraduate college, a multi-campus university (Wall Street school of education; Shrub Oak programs for Jesuit philosophers)? How was it all tied together? Some of these concerns raised questions about Jesuit control of Fordham.

Rev. Vincent O'Keefe, S.J., was president from 1963 to 1965 and as a follow-up to the Middle States report, he hired a public relations firm to assist him in exploring this question of "image." However by the time the firm's report was finished, O'Keefe had been elected to office in Rome and Rev. Leo McLaughlin, S.J., had become president of Fordham.

McLaughlin, responding to the Middle States' emphasis on changing Fordham's image from that of a seminary to that of a university, proclaimed in his inaugural address: "Fordham will pay any price, break any mold, to achieve its true function as a university."[64] What he meant by this bold statement was spelled out during the next two years and in the president's report for 1965–67, where he identified three commitments that Fordham had made: (1) to New York City, (2) to ecumenism, and (3) to educational leadership. He wrote: "We are out to prove that a Catholic university cannot exist at all if it is not great. . . . We are convinced that Fordham will not and cannot continue to exist at all unless it is great."[65]

McLaughlin's words provide a context for the rocky road traveled at Fordham from 1966 to 1969. Father Arrupe spoke at a Convocation in April 1966 celebrating the 125th anniversary of the university and encouraged Fordham in its quest for scientific probity, dialogue, and freedom, saying, in part, "Where freedom fails to flower, the University in question is no longer worthy to be called a university."[66] Despite Arrupe's words, many were distressed at McLaughlin's lack of sensitivity to Fordham's Catholic and Jesuit heritage. In retrospect it is clear that his top priority was Fordham's viability as a significant university in New York State and the freedom needed to achieve it.

In a speech at an Association of Governing Boards meeting April 17, 1967, entitled "The Changing Scene in Catholic Higher Education," McLaughlin identified four elements which characterized American Catholic higher education: (1) determination to move into the mainstream of American higher education; (2) an ecumenical thrust illustrated by Fordham's cooperative arrangments with Union Theological Seminary and the addition of Jewish and Protestant theologians to the faculty in theology at Fordham; (3) increase in lay presence on faculties, administration, and boards of trustees; and (4) transfer of ownership to a lay board of trustees.[67]

Fordham's transition would, however, have to be achieved within the political context of New York State, and that would have a significant bearing on the way in which the changes were effected. McLaughlin's predecessor, Father McGinley, was an active player at the state level, and was a leader among the Catholic institutions in the state as they joined forces with other private colleges to lobby for some kind of state aid. The Empire State Foundation, a fund-raising cooperative effort begun in the 1950s, had insisted that its members not be church-supported since that gave them an unfair advantage. Most Catholic colleges, including Fordham, had no trouble meeting that requirement. Consequently, they did not anticipate that a distinction among recipients of state funding would be made between church-related and other private institutions.

An official state program—the awarding of the Schweitzer Chair—provided an opportunity to gain funds and, perhaps even more important, prestige. Albany had awarded the chair to Fordham on behalf of H. Marshall McLuhan as a Visiting Professor of Communications for the year 1967-68, but on September 13, 1967, the attorney general of New York vetoed the assignment of the chair to Fordham on the grounds that such a grant violated the state constitution. Just at that moment the voters of New York State were being asked to ratify a revised constitution; they voted it down. Included in the proposed revision had been

the repeal of the Blaine amendment, which was the basis
for the attorney general's ruling. This amendment to the
New York State Constitution had been adopted in the nine-
teenth century and forbade the use of any state monies for
the promotion of denominational activities. Hence the
issue was whether Catholic colleges were "denominational."
This constitutional issue would be raised again in 1968 in
connection with the McGeorge Bundy Commission.

Because of the cancellation of the Schweitzer Chair
and the suspension of grants from the New York State Sci-
ence and Technology Foundation, legal counsel advised
McLaughlin in late 1967 to "alter corporate and teaching
structure so as to negative its [Fordham's] status as a denominational institution."[68] Unfortunately, Fordham—
like most other Catholic colleges in the state—had filed
a 1948 statement that it was a "religious institution." Now,
that certificate was withdrawn. The law firm also urged
Fordham to provide for true election of trustees, remove
the theology requirement for students, and hire more non-
Catholics for administration and faculty.

These recommendations were on McLaughlin's mind
when he and his executive vice president, Rev. Timothy
Healy, S.J., decided to have a serious legal study done of
Fordham's position vis-à-vis any program of state aid that
might be developed by the Regents of New York. Through
the good graces of one of the lay trustees, Fordham received
a grant from the Gerli Foundation and hired Walter Gellhorn and R. Kent Greenawalt of the Law School faculty of
Columbia University, asking them to "identify precisely, as
far as possible, measures that a prominent church-related
university might have to adopt were it to shed identification
as a religious institution in the conventional sense and, instead, gain acceptance as a completely independent institution of higher learning."[69]

Events in 1968 were decisive. As Gellhorn and Greenawalt went about their task, Governor Rockefeller and the
Regents appointed a Select Committee on Aid to Private
Higher Education. Chaired by McGeorge Bundy of the
Ford Foundation, the committee was soon known as the
Bundy Commission and the aid resulting from its work was
called the Bundy money. The importance of this particular
form of aid was that it was to be given directly to the institution without any strings attached. Based on the number
of degrees conferred each year, the grants were to become
quite substantial. The commission, on which Father Hesburgh served, explored many possibilities and considered
several options that would make the plan as equitable as
possible. Despite the defeat of the referendum on the revision of the State Constitution in the preceding November, the commission recommended the inclusion of church-
related colleges and urged the legislature to submit the
Blaine amendment by itself to a referendum for repeal.
Following the process mandated by state law, the legislature
then voted for repeal in 1968 and prepared to vote again
in 1969 (repeal required a vote in two successive legislative sessions). The Regents had already voted for repeal;
it looked as if this time the repeal effort would succeed.
Unfortunately, by the 1969 session the argument about aid
to parochial schools was once again heating up, and the legislature decided to avoid a vote on Blaine.

While awaiting any action on repeal, the legislature
voted the Bundy Commission program for aid to private
higher education into law with a provision requiring compliance with the Blaine amendment, i.e., no monies could
be given to sectarian institutions. On August 12, 1968, Commissioner Allen sent to all presidents a document entitled
"On Constitutional Eligibility pursuant to Chapter 677 of
the laws of 1968." Listed was a series of questions regarding

every aspect of the college's life. Here were spelled out the criteria by which eligibility for Bundy money would be decided. Every private college or university in the state studied them carefully to see whether or not it would qualify. Among church-related institutions the atmosphere was tense. Allen had chosen to use the criteria developed in the *Horace Mann* case, ones that led to the disqualification of three church-related schools for federal aid in Maryland in 1966.

Father Laurence McGinley, president of Fordham until 1963, was a close friend of Ewald (Joe) Nyquist, now Assistant Commissioner in New York, and had worked with him on the Middle States Commission. They had often discussed the question of aid to private higher education in New York, and McGinley thought they were in agreement on eligibility. Indeed Nyquist had indicated that Fordham might well be a first candidate. In July 1968, therefore, President McLaughlin sent one of his vice presidents, John Meng, a former president of Hunter College, to Albany to explore the developing criteria. Meng met with Robert Stone, the legal counsel in the Commissioner's office in Albany. It is not clear what transpired except that Meng reported (probably to McLaughlin) that Stone knew about the forthcoming report by Gellhorn and Greenawalt and wanted a copy when it was finished. Meng alerted Gellhorn to this request[70] and so, as the report went into final draft, it is not unlikely that the fact that Stone would receive it influenced the way it was written. Arguments which indicated the ways in which Catholic colleges and universities could qualify were highlighted in the report. The authors noted that these institutions "have become more identifiably American and less Catholic."

The Gellhorn report, as it was commonly known, was presented to the president and the board in October 1968.

It identified several changes the authors thought necessary if Fordham were to shed "its identification as a religious institution in the conventional sense and, instead, gain acceptance as a completely independent institution of higher learning"—the charge that had been given to them by President McLaughlin. One of the proposals, and the one that is most relevant to our study, was to merge the lay advisory trustees with the legal board of trustees and give the reorganized board full authority, including the appointment of the president.

Several supporting documents, including the McGrath study, were submitted in the report. In line with McGrath's thesis, the authors argued that since Fordham was incorporated in 1846 and the corporation at that time was nine non-Jesuits (a bishop, four priests, three Catholic laymen, and one Protestant layman), the property never belonged to the Jesuits. Another significant reference was to Robert Drinan, S.J., in a speech at NCEA entitled "The Constitution, Governmental Aid and Catholic higher education." Drinan was concerned about the move toward monopoly on the part of the public university establishment and he argued for united action against it, saying: "These efforts, however, probably cannot be successful, or even initiated, without a board of trustees made up of a broadly-based group of community leaders. If a board of trustees, all known leaders, speaks for a private college of which they are the governing board, their voice is far more likely to be heard than the voice of a lay or clerical faculty group from this college. . . . The creation, therefore of real decision-making boards of trustees for Catholic colleges is not only desirable but probably absolutely necessary if Catholic and other private colleges are to organize themselves and present a successful plea to legislatures and to the court of public opinion on behalf of private colleges."[71]

The Gellhorn report was not bringing entirely new ideas to the board. In April of the same year (1968), Edmund G. Ryan, S.J., who was at St. Peter's College in Jersey City and was not involved with the Bundy question except as a trustee of Fordham, had prepared a paper for the Fordham trustees concerning the McGrath thesis. Father Ryan claimed that St. Peter's was already operating on the assumption that McGrath was correct, and therefore no longer referred to superiors or to Rome for permissions. The board of trustees, he said, made the decisions—and they were all Jesuits, so the question was not so much "lay" boards as independent boards. On May 5 the Fordham board had discussed this question at length and saw the acceptance of the McGrath thesis as "another step forward" by the four Jesuit institutions in the New York province (LeMoyne, St. Peter's, Canisius, and Fordham). The trustees also favored the "Saint Louis model," and implied that they would prefer this model for Fordham if Gellhorn recommended a lay board. In the same meeting, the trustees also discussed the McGrath-Dupont study of the governance of Catholic colleges and universities.[72] They quoted with approval the suggestion that laymen be added to the board as "a way of moving toward the growing ideal of a free Christian college . . . and away from their traditions of institutions aimed largely at defending the Catholic faith."[73]

The summer of 1968 was a memorable one for many reasons. Nationally the focus was on the student demonstrations, the unruly Democratic Convention in Chicago, the civil rights conflicts, and the growing protests against the war in Vietnam. The universities were more and more drawn into the nexus of these events, and found themselves less able to exist as ivory towers. The role of universities in local communities and in the broader society was a topic of utmost concern. The logic of drawing lay persons as much as possible into the structure of Catholic colleges was convincing; the future of such institutions in a democratic society would be more viable with their support.

Consequently there were high expectations when the Gellhorn report was released on October 17, 1968. Despite the caveat in the introduction to the report—namely, that the report was a "description" of Fordham University at the close of the 1967–68 academic year and that many of its various recommendations, albeit minor, had already been implemented—and despite President McLaughlin's statement that the report would now be given to the various constituencies of the university for their review and critique, there was a public outcry that Fordham was selling its soul to get Bundy money. The headline in *The New York Times* was "End Jesuit Rule, Fordham Advised," and the Jesuit journal *America* had several articles and letters on the topic.

On October 30 the board of trustees, chaired by Rev. Michael Walsh, S.J., president of Boston College, issued a clarifying statement. Denying the interpretation that was being expressed by the critics, the board stated: "Fordham has no intention of divesting itself of its character as an independent, Catholic, and Jesuit institution of higher learning. . . . Fordham has no intention of altering its firm commitment to the maintenance of an outstanding department of theology within the university, or of abandoning any of its objectives as a Catholic and Jesuit university operating within the American education tradition." Further, those changes which had already been made at Fordham were "made independent of the study and were based on decisions made in line with sound contemporary educational policy and with the post-Vatican II spirit and orientations at work within the Catholic Church. *They were not made to gain legal parity for the reception of public aid* [emphasis mine]."[74]

This statement was sent to the twenty-nine bishops of New York State, the presidents of all Catholic colleges and universities, and the national offices of NCEA, ACE, and JEA. Obviously there was need to pour water on the fires that had been ignited. Internally, the various "constituencies" that McLauglin had referred to did indeed consider the Gellhorn report and some offered criticism. One report (possibly done by Father McGinley, the former president) charged that Gellhorn contained errors of fact; contrary to the report, the university and the community were already separately incorporated and the trustees did elect and remove the president. Fordham's legal counsel, Caesar Pitassy, noted that it would be important to check with the state attorney general to make sure that the changes which were being suggested would, in fact, make Fordham eligible for state aid. Despite mounting criticism, President McLaughlin nevertheless congratulated Gellhorn on "a wonderful job" and said that he saw this as "resolving the church-state relationship which has plagued institutions."[75]

Perhaps the strongest denunciation of the report came from Edwin A. Quain, S.J., director of the Fordham University Press. A distinguished member of the university faculty and academic vice president from 1952 to 1956, he refused to print the report. In a memo of October 31, he wrote: "In twenty-seven years of reading dissertations and term papers, I have turned down applicants for degrees and course credit for defects less serious than this failure in scholarly method."[76] In May 1969 Gellhorn was given permission to publish the report himself, and in a rather curt note of November 26, 1969, the new Fordham president, Rev. Michael Walsh, S.J., declined an offer from Gellhorn to provide extra copies by saying that those who needed it already had mimeographed copies! Obviously, the report had turned out to be a public relations disaster.

Walsh had been elected president by the trustees in December 1968.[77] That summer a petition had been submitted to the New York State Regents to enlarge the board to up to thirty-one trustees. The permission was received in February 1969 and shortly thereafter, a new board was announced. Mr. Joseph A. Kaiser, a layman, was elected as chair of the reconstituted board with eleven Jesuits and fifteen laymen as its first members; Fordham's president was the sole *ex officio* member. The Jesuits who were asked to serve were a distinguished group in higher education, including John Donohue, Avery Dulles, Robert Mitchell, Donald Monan, Edmund Ryan, Terrence Toland, Victor Yanitelli, and Donald Campion—a clear signal to others of the importance placed on continuing Jesuit influence despite the lessening of "control." However, the new bylaws did not specify any particular mix of laymen and religious on the board. The president of Fordham would be chosen by a majority of the board of trustees rather than by a religious authority. The bylaws did not limit the board's choice of the president in any way. Thus, within a short time after Walsh took office, governance changes had been made and Fordham University was now independent of the Society of Jesus.[78]

The president's report for 1968–69 summarized the tumultuous events of the year in an understated manner: "The university's system of governance was changed significantly when the Board of Trustees was enlarged to include a majority of lay men." The report reviewed the history of the board, explaining the existence of a board of lay advisory trustees since 1958 and the petition sent to Albany in 1968 to enlarge the legal board. The reason given for this action was the "growing complexity and diversity" of the university. A separate corporation had been developed for the religious community, and the Jesuit residences had been transferred to that corporation. The Jesuit faculty members would now seek university appointments through regular channels and agreements on salary and tenure were being developed.[79]

The contrast between the Saint Louis story and that of Fordham is striking. In both cases there was a desire to move the university into the mainstream of American higher education and to create a new image for the institution. The change to an independent board of trustees was one step in the process, but the external circumstances dictated the way it happened. Having participated in the May 1967 meeting at Saint Louis and discussed with the other Jesuit presidents the reasons for laicization of the board, Leo McLaughlin might have been able to achieve his goal without turmoil if the Gellhorn study and the issue of Bundy money had not intervened. The concurrence of Father Arrupe in the arrangements made by the Saint Louis community and the general climate in Catholic universities may well have given McLaughlin reason to think he was simply acting in an expected manner. But the public perception that Gellhorn's recommendations for achieving eligibility for the Bundy money meant a denial of Fordham's Catholic and Jesuit heritage was a death blow to the career of Leo McLaughlin. No amount of later explanation could fully repair the damage.

While Catholic college presidents across the country were quoting the Land O'Lakes document to reinforce their arguments for "academic freedom and institutional autonomy" and to explain why lay presence on their boards would be an asset, it was the simultaneous effort to qualify for eligibility for the Bundy money which caused the negative reaction on the part of Fordham alumni and their friends to the changes McLaughlin initiated. Unfortunately, his public utterances were not reassuring, but rather fanned the flames of opposition by their imprudence and even recklessness. McLaughlin's speeches were quoted everywhere to suggest that the only priority at Fordham was to be a great university, and this would be done no matter what the cost in terms of its heritage.

The political fiasco at Fordham became a rallying cry for those in other institutions who were opposed to the idea of having laymen on the boards. Several of the Jesuit colleges which were moving in that direction slowed down. Despite the paper of Father Ryan on "Secularization," prepared for the Fordham board and probably utilized by others, an inherent link was perceived between the move to lay boards and the denial of Catholic heritage in order to become "secular." Unfortunately, Fordham was seen as the prime example of what could happen when the religious decided to surrender control.

In 1969 Fordham, Manhattanville, and St. John Fisher were the only Catholic colleges declared eligible for Bundy money. Later on, other Catholic colleges, New Rochelle, Iona, Canisius, and Marymount-Manhattan, would sue New York State, questioning the perceived differences between themselves and the first group. Costly litigation led to eventual reception of Bundy money on the part of all of the Catholic colleges that applied for it. But in the meantime the public image of Fordham, as the one who first broke the barrier, suffered. The controversial link between the Gellhorn report and the eligibility of Fordham for the Bundy

money overshadowed the careful distinction made by Fordham in its presentation to Albany, when seeking Bundy aid,
that it was nonsectarian but not secular.[80] Such a distinction
was certainly not grasped by the public. In the years that
followed, Fordham and the other Catholic colleges in
New York State would be trapped in an ambiguity about
their Catholic identity. At Fordham, no amount of docu-
mentation demonstrating that many of the decisions to
make changes were made prior to the Gellhorn report could
dispel the popular misconception that the Gellhorn report
made Fordham secular. Unfortunately, the shift in the legal
control of the university by the addition of lay persons to
the board of trustees in 1969 was associated in the public
mind with the trend toward secularization. A reading of the
minutes of the board, however, makes it clear that nothing could be further from the truth. The election of Rev.
Michael Walsh, S.J., brought an end to the McLaughlin era
and strengthened commitment to the fact that Fordham
was not a "secular" university. The new lay board would
work with Walsh at being Jesuit and Catholic, whatever the
legal terminology prescribed.

The seven different Catholic institutions that we have
studied in detail—New Rochelle, Saint Louis, Notre
Dame, Mundelein, Portland, Saint Michael's, and Fordham—illustrate how different the process of laicization was
on each campus, and how varied were the results. At some
places there was a great deal of discussion about the importance of the laity in the church, at others the focus was on
becoming centers of academic excellence and consequently,
the need for lay support and increased resources; at still
others, there was more concern about eligibility for federal
and state funding and the need for greater contact with the
surrounding community. The numbers of religious and the

attitudes they had toward higher education also influenced the arguments for laicization. For all, however, a fundamental desire was to separate the college from the religious community's administration and authority, and by 1970 such independence was achieved.

THREE

Legal Concerns

An examination of the process followed by individual Catholic colleges and universities in creating new
structures of government for their institutions during the
late 1960s inevitably uncovers the "McGrath thesis" as a
critical canonical resource.[1] With amazing alacrity and un-
animity, the proponents of the creation of fully independent boards of trustees relied on the canonical opinions
of Rev. John McGrath, a relatively unknown canon lawyer
at The Catholic University of America. This reliance certainly suggests that his thesis was perceived as crucial in
trying to bring about a shift in governing power from religious communities to separate boards of trustees, generally
composed of both lay and religious members.

In 1966 the Court of Appeals in Maryland handed down
the decision in the *Horace Mann* case, which held uncon-
stitutional the state grants to two Catholic colleges on the
grounds that they were "sectarian."[2] This raised significant
questions among civil and constitutional lawyers about the
relationship between religious communities and Catholic
colleges and universities. We will therefore need to review
briefly the history and status of the institutions vis-à-vis
both state and church to appreciate the legal questions involved in the move to independent boards.

In this chapter we will consider the McGrath thesis, the
Horace Mann and the *Tilton* cases, the reactions to these
canonical and civil opinions, the ways that Catholic colleges
and universities accommodated to these legal realities, and
the problems that consequently developed in their relationship with church authorities, particularly in Rome.

Historical Background

At the time of their foundation, most of the Catholic colleges had received charters from the various state governments enabling them to offer the appropriate higher education degrees. Sometimes these charters named lay persons as trustees, at other times, a mixture of clerical and lay. But in still other cases, the religious community which already had a charter for its corporate legal existence simply extended its reach to the activities of a college, and no new corporation was formed.[3] Whatever the statutory situation, the "legal trustees" fulfilled the responsibilities that were required by law: approval of transactions concerning finances and real estate; official awarding of all degrees; and approval of appointed officers and trustees. But regardless of the corporate form, all decisions were actually subject to the will of the religious community leadership. I have not discovered any truly independent lay governing board prior to the 1960s. Usually the lay boards, where they existed, had no decision-making power in regard to the curriculum, discipline, admission of students, or the hiring and firing of faculty. Those powers were exercised by the appointed officials of the religious community, some of whom were also the administrators and/or faculty of the college. Where there was no separate corporation formed for the college, the trustees were generally the members of the council of the religious community acting *ex officio* as trustees; even when there was a separate corporation, the role of the community council was significant in the affairs of the college. In diocesan colleges, the control was exercised by the local Ordinary with the assistance of a board of lay and clerical members whose function was consultative.

It was not, in fact, until 1963 that any Catholic university was founded with an explicit intention of being governed by laymen. Sacred Heart University, in Bridgeport, Connecticut, had a board of three clergymen and two laymen, and the administration was exclusively laymen. The university was sponsored by the diocese of Bridgeport, which was commended by the pope for having placed the institution in the hands of the laity.[4]

Canon Law Perspectives

In 1965 the governing structures of Catholic colleges were anything but uniform. They did, however, have many features in common. Because the colleges were understood to be the apostolic work of a religious community or diocese, the rules governing church property were generally followed. The acquisition of new land, erection of buildings, or sale of properties were generally the subject of referral to religious authorities for authorization. It was assumed that the religious administering the institutions would seek the needed permissions from local or provincial authorities and they, in turn, would often have to submit the proposal to a General Council and perhaps also to a Roman Congregation for approbation. Instances are cited in the minutes of the boards where permission is sought and granted on a regular basis. It seems safe to say that, correctly or not, college authorities acted as if their institutions were canonically accountable.

As Catholic higher education expanded, especially after World War II and the subsequent legislation granting aid to students and institutions of higher education, such "permission-seeking" became an obstacle to rapid and independent decision-making and to the setting of long-range priorities. To secure loans from government sources it was important that the "collateral" was not held in the name of a religious community. Most colleges had by then established boards of lay advisors (under several different titles) to assist with fund-raising and management expertise, and their advice was welcomed by the presidents. Troublesome tensions arose, however, when the lay persons who raised the funds found that they had little to say about how such monies would be spent. Businessmen and civil lawyers were not accustomed to the canonical way of life and found themselves hemmed in by regulations and permissions. Ordinarily they did not complain about this, since their main purpose was to help the university and the community that ran it, but dissatisfaction was inevitable. As time went on, the presidents found themselves in the middle of a growing conflict of interest. As members of the religious community, they knew the canonical world, but, as presidents of expanding universities, they also knew the limitations that such parameters placed on their aspirations. The anecdote concerning Father Hesburgh and the lawnmower cited in the first chapter was a symbol of the problem that he and his presidential colleagues were having with a cumbersome system of governance.

A proposed ecclesial solution to this dilemma surfaced just at the right time. In 1965 Father John McGrath of The Catholic University of America began to make the rounds of Catholic college meetings, presenting his ideas about property that was held "in trust" at Catholic institutions. In the next few years he was a featured speaker at several important gatherings, notably the May 1967 meeting of all Jesuit presidents and some of their lawyers at Saint Louis University, and a meeting of Jesuit provincials in October of that same year. In February 1968 he was one of the key participants at a conference on governance held at Loretto Heights.[5]

McGrath's work, funded by the Raskob foundation, was published in 1968 and was strongly supported by the NCEA College and University Department and by its executive director, Father Clarence Friedman.[6] McGrath's influence can be seen in the many positive references to his thesis by those developing new boards. He was cited in the Gellhorn report at Fordham, by Reinert, Hesburgh, and Ann Ida Gannon in their arguments for independent boards in 1967, and by Dupont at Saint Michael's the following year. Mc-Grath's opinion had already been relied upon in 1966 in the arguments for the establishment of the independent board at the College of New Rochelle, where legal counsel, Charles Horgan, cited it as reason why there were no canonical impediments to complete lay governance.[7]

As a civil lawyer, Horgan saw in McGrath the answer to the knotty questions of canon law which had arisen in recent years as a result of academic freedom conflicts and questions of eligibility for government funds. Were these institutions and their properties owned by the Catholic church? If the colleges could demonstrate that they were not "owned" or "controlled" by the church, would their independence be recognized by secular authorities? If laymen constituted a majority of the governing board, would the colleges still be considered "Catholic"? Was church property being alienated when a majority of laymen were elected to a board previously composed of all or, at least, a majority of religious? Who really owned these Catholic colleges and universities? Who should control them? By what law were they to be governed, canon, civil, or both?

Now, in the light of proposals to share power more completely with the laity, there was good reason to stress the opinion that, in fact, the canonical rules governing property did not pertain to institutions which were "owned and operated" not by religious communities but by private legal corporations. McGrath thus contributed a significant legal framework for the argument against the need for an indult of alienation when properties and governance were transferred to independent boards of trustees.

One of the issues raised at Saint Louis University during the discussions concerning such a transfer was directly connected to this point. Rather than accepting the McGrath thesis, Father James O'Connor, S.J., himself a canon lawyer, argued for a specific bylaw that would bind lay trustees to the canon law. In a paper given to the Jesuit presidents in June 1966, O'Connor set forth his convictions on this point.[8] While he did not oppose the movement to include more laymen on the boards, he did disagree with it on the status of the property used by the colleges. He relied on canon 1497 (Code of 1917) for his definition of church property: "Temporal goods, whether movable or immovable corporeal or incorporeal goods, which belong to the Church universal and the Apostolic See, or to some other moral person in the Church are ecclesiastical goods or Church property." He further argued that "the right to own and to administer property in a religious institute derives from the will of a still higher authority, namely, the Church." O'Connor spoke of the "stewardship of God's patrimony" as a solemn obligation of the religious institute, and argued that while the administration of the property could be arranged in a variety of ways, the ownership could not simply be transferred.

O'Connor offered three solutions to the problem he saw in the participation of lay persons on the board of trustees: (1) place a majority of religious on the board so that by voting as a bloc, their control would be assured; however, he recognized that this might create a conflict of conscience for individuals when the good of the college appeared opposed to the good of the community or the wishes of religious authority;[9] (2) create two corporations with one, composed of members of the religious order, for ownership and the other, allowing lay members, for management; (3) include a special bylaw which would read: "All members of the Board of Trustees, singly and jointly, bind themselves to the observance not only of the requirements of civil law but also to all requirements of canon law." O'Connor said that he was proposing the last simply as a theoretical solution and that, as far as he knew, no one had adopted it.

O'Connor's proposed solutions were discussed at the May 1967 meeting, although by that time they had already been rejected by the leadership which had designed the new board at Saint Louis University. O'Connor may, however, have influenced the thinking of some of the other Jesuit presidents or of Father Arrupe because his second solution was adopted by some Jesuit institutions. Others leaned toward the first solution, although they may have discovered that the caveat offered by O'Connor was an important one. I do not know of any that adopted the third suggestion, although there may be some who at least considered it.

McGrath, on the other hand, spoke to the presidents' need for some kind of ecclesiastical affirmation of their efforts to set up predominantly lay boards with full and legal governing authority. For a decade or so they had sought for ways of increasing the role of lay advisory trustees because of their financial expertise and their contacts in the business world but had been hampered by the need to limit their authority over the financial affairs of the university.

Using McGrath's thesis, college presidents could justify their plans for the reorganization of the boards in terms which dealt with the objections from members of their religious communities who often saw what was happening as a "give-away" of the institute's resources. Basing his views on an examination of the history of American Catholic colleges and universities (as well as hospitals) and their status in civil law, McGrath claimed that these institutions clearly existed to serve a public purpose so that, although founded as apostolic works, they always had to consider both their public and religious purposes.

Since the civil law had not required incorporation of the works of the community separate from that of the incorporation of the religious community itself, the affairs of the two entities had often become intermingled in a way that led to a lack of clear authority and accountability. In the new circumstances created by the separation of the college from the community, how would authority be exercised by an independent board of trustees, and to whom would the trustees be accountable if the community no longer "owned" the college?

Such a problem disappeared, however, if one subscribed to McGrath's basic argument that the institution had never been a "juridic person" in canon law and that therefore the property it had acquired had never been ecclesiastical property. The community had never "owned" the university; the corporation had. He argued: "The property, real and personal, of Catholic hospitals and educational institutions which have been incorporated as American law corporations is the property of the corporate entity and not the property of the sponsoring body or individuals who conduct the institutions. . . . There is no question of dealing with ecclesiastical property when speaking of the property of Catholic hospitals and higher educational institutions in the United States." He continued: "The canon law is clear that property is ecclesiastical only when it belongs to some ecclesiastical moral person. Since the institutions under consideration have not themselves been established as moral persons and, since no other moral person in fact holds title to the property of the institution, their assets are not ecclesiastical property."[10]

When McGrath moved to the question being posed regarding the future canonical status of institutions under the auspices of the Catholic church, and when he tried to deal with the issue of a continued identity as "Catholic" once the colleges became objects of governance by lay people rather than by a religious community, he proved to be quite conservative. In the second part of his work, his opinion about the religious community's future role was not very different from that of O'Connor; McGrath, too, thought it was imperative to keep the religious in a position of control and authority even after adding laymen to the board. McGrath was clear that in his view the colleges were not "church property" in the sense of canon law; yet he supported the continued control of the institution by the religious community, and suggested various ways that this could be implemented within the civil law that governed corporations.

McGrath suggested several channels through which influence could be exercised, namely, through charter and bylaws, the board of trustees, administration, and staff. While he denied the legal claims of the canonists that the property was "church property," he insisted that the bylaws could secure the influence of the sponsoring body. Describing an ideal Catholic college, he said: "The influence of the sponsoring body is reflected strongly in the by-laws, and provision is made for a definite number of the board of directors to be chosen from the sponsoring body. The by-laws usually state the nature of the institution and the Catholic influences that inspired its foundation. The board of trustees is entrusted with the obligation to manage the affairs of the institution in keeping with these Catholic traditions." He further suggested that the bylaws could require the board of trustees to choose the president and other officers of the institution from members of the sponsoring body.[11]

McGrath did not suggest a new legal structure which would eliminate all influence by the founding community but rather envisioned a new "cooperative separateness." Nevertheless, to those who were desirous of separating the administration of the university from the authority of the religious community, McGrath furnished the perfect starting point. In most cases, the achievement of "separateness" required that a new civil corporation be established for the religious community since the "corporation" in existence was that of the university. Even though the trustees of that corporation were members of the religious community, in McGrath's opinion it was the corporate personality of the university that "owned" the institution and not the religious community.[12] In certain other cases, the original and only corporation was that of the religious community at the college or of the province, so there was need for a new civil corporation for the college if separation were to be achieved. Although unusual, there were a few instances where two separate corporations already existed: one for the college and one for the religious community.

Another noteworthy aspect of McGrath's thesis had to do with the questions of ownership and trusteeship in American civil law. It was his opinion, although later challenged, that "the public" held "equitable title" to the assets of the corporation although the corporation held legal title to them. His reason was that it is the general public that is served by charitable corporations and hence, in case of dissolution, such property is ordinarily distributed to another charitable corporation of similar purpose. Accepting this legal opinion meant that the religious community would not necessarily be the beneficiary were the college or university to cease operations. McGrath suggested that the religious community should stop using language that signified "owning and operating" the institution.[13] The board of trustees, whether lay or religious or some combination thereof, held the property "in trust" and was accountable to the appropriate state bodies and not to religious authorities. It should no longer be considered a part of the ecclesiastical scheme of things but should be seen as an independent corporate reality operating "under the auspices" of a religious community or diocese.

The dozen or so diocesan colleges do not appear to have been affected by the McGrath thesis as much as those linked to religious communities. That may be because their boards were already a mixture of lay and clerical members, and the clear understanding was that they *assisted* the local bishop, generally the chair of the board, to carry out his responsibilities. Some diocesan colleges were separately incorporated while others were simply part of the "corporation sole."[14]

Although Father Hesburgh was originally hesitant about the McGrath thesis, he came to support it. Nevertheless, the Procurator General of Holy Cross, Father Heston (himself a canon lawyer), thought that the university was indeed ecclesiastical property and consequently sought an indult of alienation in 1967, which was easily obtained in the spirit of post-Vatican II regard for the role of the laity. At Saint Louis University, on the other hand, Father Reinert decided not to seek an indult of alienation and was supported in this position by both his provincial, Rev. Linus Thro, and the Father General, Father Arrupe. The other Jesuit colleges and many women's colleges made the same decision and indults were never requested for the actions taken.

McGrath was not only a speaker at public meetings but also visited many campuses during 1966 and 1967. Trustee minutes and internal memoranda at several colleges reveal that he was the most frequently quoted authority when the proposal for lay boards was on the table. Unfortunately, McGrath died at an early age in 1970 and could no longer engage in the later discussion. As might be surmised, it was most often not the lay trustees who cited him, except for a few civil lawyers; it was the priests and religious anxious to bring about what they regarded as genuine reform who invoked his name.

Were there contemporary critics of the McGrath thesis? According to Rev. Robert Kennedy, a distinguished canonist at The Catholic University of America, the thesis received almost no notice in law journals of the period.[15] Attention was paid to the McGrath thesis in more general publications such as *America* in the years 1968–70, and there the comments were generally favorable.

However, within university circles the McGrath thesis did encounter a few serious critics. At the January 1967 chapter held at Notre Dame, strong reservations were expressed about McGrath's propositions by Brother Raymond Fleck, C.S.C., president of St. Edward's University, and Father Louis J. Thornton, C.S.C., of the Notre Dame community. In Jesuit circles, we have already noted the opposing view of Father James O'Connor. A paper presented by Father John Ford, S.J., to a meeting of Jesuits at Round Hill on May 26, 1967 contains some further reservations based on the undue haste with which the changes in governance were being made. He stressed the fundamental concern which he and his brother Jesuits were experiencing about the sharing of responsibility with laymen in a way that might give the laity ultimate control of the university. What effect would it have on their own Jesuit apostolate in higher education? Because their vocation was carried on in a context of both canon and civil law, the decision being considered was a very basic one. To Ford there was a very real conflict of laws concerning these institutions, and he insisted that in such a case the sovereignty of the church over her own affairs must be recognized. While Ford said that he was not opposed to the changes being made, he thought it very important that all the ramifications of the decision be understood. A questionnaire had been distributed to all participants at the Round Hill meeting, and in his own answers to the questions, Ford made it clear that he feared that if a schism were to occur (and in post-Vatican II days that was not an unrealistic fear), Jesuit properties would no longer be on the side of the pope. But property aside, his basic worry was that the seat of government was shifting from church to civil authorities; this meant that the university would not be a Catholic or Jesuit institution because its basic authority would be understood to derive from the charter granted by civil authority and vested in a board of trustees, without due regard for its origin in the church. For such a radical change in juridical governing power, he considered permission from the General of the Society and the Holy See to be essential. Perhaps his sharpest comment was that Father Reinert, in speaking simply of "enlarging the Board of Trustees" as his goal, was avoiding the fact that "in the concrete [there is] an acknowledgment that the civil law is ultimately controlling."[16]

A few years later, Ruth Cessna, attorney for the Jesuit community at San Francisco, was asked by Jesuit authorities

to do a critique of McGrath for circulation among the presidents of the Jesuit institutions. The title of her 1971 paper,
"John J. McGrath: The Mask of Divestiture and Disaffiliation," suggests her conclusions.[17] Her analysis cited
many weaknesses in McGrath's position, and she especially
disagreed with his understanding of the constitutional and
civil law provisions regarding the guarantee of protection of
private property. She concluded that "The ownership of
Catholic institutions is exactly where it has always been—
in the Church." She strongly criticized those she called
"separatists" who were using McGrath's thesis to justify "institutional secularism via the corporate purpose."

In response to the express desire of the Father General to
study the Cessna paper, the Jesuit presidents entrusted this
task to Father Dexter Hanley, S.J., who, in turn, consulted
the legal counsels of the twenty-eight schools. According to his memo to the Association of Jesuit Colleges
and Universities Board of Governors, January 8, 1972, the
legal counsels of twenty-one Jesuit colleges had evaluated
Cessna's work and "it is the unanimous opinion of legal
counsel that the Cessna thesis is erroneous and misleading."
The "counsel of the several universities unanimously conclude that Miss Cessna's position is untenable, and that the
McGrath position is substantially correct."[18] This response
provided by Hanley clearly supported the basic argument
that religious communities do not "own" the colleges, nor is
the property "church property," and in case of dissolution of
the corporation it would not revert to the Society of Jesus or
the Church.

While I do not wish to enter into the merits of Miss
Cessna's legal arguments nor of Father Hanley's counter-
arguments, I do find it noteworthy that the twenty-eight
Jesuit presidents approved this critique of her thesis on

the very day it was presented to them, and without any recorded substantial discussion. Hanley's criticism of the Cessna thesis was then forwarded to the provincials and Father Arrupe. Father Hanley added some comments about the way in which Jesuits could still influence the university despite recognition of the "public trust" nature of the institution.

Also on record is a memo from William J. Gibbons to Rev. John Fitterer, S.J., AJCU president, dated January 26, 1972, responding to Hanley's critique.[19] Gibbons was not so sanguine about the Hanley position and pointed out that seven of the Jesuit university counsels did not respond to Hanley's request for comments and may have not been in agreement with it. Gibbons claimed that McGrath slighted some broader jurisprudential and constitutional principles. He thought that some court decisions on which McGrath relied might in the future be overturned and that a more critical study of the whole matter was needed.

Those who had reservations about McGrath's legal opinion seem to have been voices crying in the wilderness. It was clearly the McGrath line of reasoning that guided the decisions made by the colleges in the late 1960s and 1970s.[20] By 1977, as the Stamm study showed, approximately 75 percent of the colleges had altered their governance structures by adding controlling numbers of lay persons to their boards.[21] While McGrath had not urged that all control of institutional policy be surrendered by religious communities to the new boards, he did set the stage for arguments to that effect. Others would use his work to argue that if the assets had a "public" character and were held in trust by the board of trustees and not by the religious community as such, it followed logically that the board (whatever proportion of lay and religious members) should exercise full authority over the life of the university. It was further adduced that the presidents, in being accountable to the board alone and not to canonical superiors, were now presiding over institutions that recognized the source of their legal authority in the state rather than in the church.

Civil Law

There can be no doubt that another significant factor in the rapid transformation of the governance structures was the June 2, 1966 decision in the Maryland case known as *Horace Mann League v Board of Public Works of Maryland*. This case concerned the constitutionality of grants for construction of dormitory and classroom facilities at church-related colleges. Two of the four defendants were Catholic institutions (College of Notre Dame and St. Joseph's College), and the Maryland Court of Appeals ruled against them because they were "legally sectarian." When the Supreme Court refused to hear an appeal, a wave of anxiety swept through the church-related sector. Although at the moment only applicable in the state of Maryland, the criteria used by the Maryland courts to determine "sectarianism" were indeed threatening.

These criteria were six: (1) the stated purpose of the college; (2) the religious affiliations of the college's personnel; (3) the college's relationship with religious organizations and groups; (4) the place of religion in the college's program; (5) the long-range impact or outcome of the college program on its graduates; and (6) the work and image of the college in the local community. For our current study of governing structures, the important ones concerned the makeup of the board of trustees and its relationship to the religious community. The second criterion included the religious affiliations of members of the governing board. Were the religious members "controlling" the decisions of the board? Was there a requirement that members be of a particular faith or church?

Even before the final decision was announced, an extremely forthright address was delivered at the NCEA convention in April 1966. Francis X. Gallagher, a Baltimore lawyer who had represented the Catholic colleges in the *Horace Mann* case, laid some of the blame for the view that their institutions were sectarian on the Catholic colleges themselves. In general, he maintained, they were overzealous in their claims about their Catholicity in brochures and catalogues.[22] He was particularly angered at the constant use of the word "permeating" as a way of describing the distinctive character of Catholic higher education. The colleges themselves claimed, he said, that the Catholic faith "permeated" everything from chemistry to gym classes, in fact, the entire atmosphere. To Gallagher, this language was a "Trojan horse," for it gave evidence to the plaintiffs that indeed the Catholic colleges were "sectarian." The term "permeation," he argued, is "ill defined and ill used." Furthermore, the control of the colleges was indeed still in the hands of religious orders and this clearly raised a constitutional issue. "Certainly, the selection of a president of a Catholic college in actuality is little more than a corporate exercise calling for the placing of a civil stamp of approval on the decision of a religious general or superior. . . . The texts of the Rules of religious communities are used [presumably by the opposition] against the argument that the colleges are in practice quite free for they speak of the 'blind obedience' of the religious to the superior." The purpose of the college, when still stated "in old-world educational jargon," was a real handicap, and Gallagher suggested that all of these documents should be over-hauled. In effect, he was urging that the presidents clean up the language in their publications and in the documents of the religious order so that the plaintiffs in future cases would not have the same deadly weapons in their hands.

While the McGrath theory gave food for thought and legal speculation, the *Horace Mann* decision put the issue squarely on the table with an urgency that had significant concrete results. Its potential as a precedent in other decisions regarding government funding seemed unlimited. It was not long before such a domino effect began. The New York State department of education adopted the criteria used in *Horace Mann* as the basis for declaring eligibility for the new grants under the Aid to Private Higher Education law of 1968 (Bundy money).[23]

In responding to this challenge, the Catholic colleges and universities in New York rewrote their bylaws, eliminating any reference to control by the religious community or ecclesiastical authorities. None of them seem to have included "corporate Members" with reserved powers concerning appointments and properties or mission, and none are explicit about the number of members from the religious community who will serve as trustees. I have also not found any which required the president to be a member of the sponsoring religious community or, indeed, to be a Catholic.[24] One might say that in New York, the McGrath thesis came to its logical conclusion; as institutions serving a public purpose and regarding their assets as a "public trust," the colleges and universities henceforth found their locus of authority in civil power and not in the church.

Actually, the New York colleges went beyond McGrath, for in the second part of his treatise (one not often referred to at the time) McGrath, as we have seen, saw no reason why the bylaws should not safeguard the rights of the religious community by providing for a certain number of trustees from the community and requiring that the president and other officers be members of the sponsoring group. In stressing the separateness of the community and the institution it founded, McGrath did not urge breaking off a relationship which had been so fruitful, and yet such a rupture was bound to follow. Control of the college by religious authority was, as *Horace Mann* demonstrated, not a viable option if federal or state funding were needed. In addition, the recognition that the institution was rooted in the state's power to grant charters for educational purposes increased the college's spirit of independence from the religious community. Unfortunately, McGrath failed to suggest a canonical or civil model for a partnership of equals, a need that arose from his theory of the college as a "public trust." If laity were to govern the institutions of Catholic higher education and if they were, by definition, not subject to the canon law regarding property, what could be the new relationship between the institutions and the church? Responding to this question would be the work of the next few decades in Catholic higher education.

New Forms of Partnership

In 1967 both Saint Louis and Notre Dame attempted to answer this question when they set up independent boards of trustees. They both had as a goal the continuation of influence on the part of the religious community after control had been ceded to the new board. The mechanism used at Notre Dame was the creation of a separate entity, the Fellows, a group of twelve trustees, half laymen and half Holy Cross priests but all very committed to the mission of the university. To the Fellows was given responsibility for safe-guarding the Catholic mission, the selection of trustees and officers, and sale or transfer of properties. The Fellows delegated authority to the board of trustees, except for those matters directly related to their specific responsibilities.

At Saint Louis University the strategy was different. In the new bylaws of 1967 provision was made for a so-called "Jesuit veto," without ever using that term. This meant that the decisions concerning university property and the basic Jesuit mission could not be made without a two-thirds vote, and over one-third of the full board were to be Jesuits. This concept of a "Jesuit veto" served as an important point for Father Reinert when he opposed seeking an indult of alienation for the transfer of governance. It is interesting to note that this "veto" was never used. At a meeting in April, 1974, the board amended the bylaws to allow from twenty-five to forty trustees with a minimum of eleven Jesuits. This ended the so-called Jesuit veto. There was some criticism of this bylaw amendment because it represented a loss of symbolic "Jesuitness."[25]

Other mechanisms for guaranteeing the influence of the religious community were also developed in the years following McGrath and *Horace Mann*. While some institutions simply relied on the commitment of the lay trustees to the Catholic mission of the university and their remarkable dedication to its well-being, others were not so sanguine. A variety of structures were adopted by religious congregations to guarantee their continued influence after adding laymen to the board.

In his 1977 study, Martin Stamm identified eight models of governance among Catholic colleges and universities. The basic distinction he made was between a unicameral form, which meant that there was only one governing body, the board of trustees, and it "exercised all the corporate functions unilaterally and independently," and a bicameral configuration, among which he identified five different models. In all of the bicameral models, a distinct corporation was created with certain reserved powers, generally those regarding property, the mission of the institution, and selection of president and/or trustees. The Members of this corporation were often *ex officio* the governing council of the religious community. Stamm considered both unicameral and bicameral arrangements under the general umbrella of "independent corporate systems"; only those very few colleges which were governed by a religious community council as part of a corporate arrangement including other apostolic institutions sponsored by that community were considered by him as "dependent."

In 1977, according to Stamm, 91 percent of the 134 institutions in his study had some form of "independent corporate system," with 60 percent falling in the unicameral class and the remaining 31 percent in the bicameral class. His follow-up study of 125 institutions in 1992 found 96 percent with an independent corporate stucture, including 57 percent with the unicameral and 39 percent with the two-tier, or bicameral, arrangement. While he noted a continuing increase in the number of lay persons on the boards, he also pointed out that almost half of the institutions reporting in 1992 cited a change in their corporate structure since 1977. Unfortunately, the direction of the change was not given. Further study needs to be done to find out if these revisions were significant.[26]

In 1971, a less restrictive interpretation of the "separation" clause of the United States constitution was set forth by the Supreme Court in the *Tilton v Richardson* case. Mr. Charles Wilson, the attorney of record for Edward Bennett Williams who represented the four Connecticut Catholic colleges involved in that suit, has suggested that if the Supreme Court's *Tilton* decision, with its more lenient position toward church-related institutions, had come sooner, it might have slowed down the movement to independent, particularily unicameral, boards.[27] However, as others perceive it, the threat was still there even after *Tilton*. For while the original Connecticut court ruling in *Tilton* was overturned by the Supreme Court in the colleges' favor, it was a five to four decision and it was limited to the four schools in question. No general policy about the eligibility of church-related colleges for federal or state funds could be inferred. The Catholic colleges and universities, however, were encouraged by the support shown to them by their colleagues in higher education, signifying the extent to which they were now accepted as equals. An amicus brief was submitted in the *Tilton* case by the American Council on Education, the Association of American Colleges, the National Association of State Universities and Land-grant Colleges, the Association of American Universities, and the Council for the Advancement of Small Colleges.

Tilton had a double effect: it meant that there could be no further legal challenge to the "non-sectarian" character of Catholic higher education in general, since plaintiffs would have to sue individual institutions (approximately 250 at this time); but it also meant that there would be long-term ambiguity about the Catholic identity of many institutions. According to *Tilton*, if certain characteristics of an individual college were found to be "sectarian" the institution would be in danger of losing funds, but the court gave no clear guidance on exactly what those characteristics might be. The administration of the four Connecticut Catholic colleges had been required to answer questions about their religious heritage, symbols, and programs. Answers which did not reject a college's Catholic commitment could easily entrap the college in a charge of sectarianism.

To a certain extent Wilson's question about the speed with which the colleges moved to independence can be answered affirmatively. The urgency that was felt by the leaders, especially between 1967 and 1971, was certainly linked to the fear that they would not meet the eligibility criteria for funding, and since one of the categories examined in both *Horace Mann* and *Tilton* concerned the makeup of the board of trustees and the possibility that its power over the institution's policies was subject to a religious organization, presidents were naturally anxious to present to the public a board that was clearly "independent." However, it is my opinion that the many reasons unrelated to the constitutionality of government funding would still have mandated the change, although perhaps rather more slowly. Presidents and lay advisory trustees in the 1960s needed to adapt their governance structures to the realities of day-to-day administration. Increasing crises over faculty and student rights and responsibilities called for decision-making processes that were clear and open. While the issue of canonical accountability may have been important to some canonists, there was strong support from religious superiors and bishops for the colleges to do what they needed in order to advance in the circles of higher education. If the shift to independent boards in order to qualify for government funds had been perceived by the bishops as a prelude to "secularization," it is unlikely that they would have contributed as much as they did to the fund to support the Connecticut colleges in the *Tilton* case.[28] It was not long before the "independent" nature of the board came to be taken for granted by church authorities as well as by religious communities.[29]

As a matter of fact, I have found no evidence that the addition of lay persons to boards of trustees brought a "secularizing" atmosphere to the university or college. While it is true that one of the fears voiced in the days when the changes were being made was that adding a majority of lay persons to the boards would mean the secularization of Catholic universities and colleges, no one has demonstrated a causal connection. In the discussions at the seven institutions studied here the issue was frequently raised, but the argument seemed to run counter to the ecclesiology of Vatican II in that it implied that lay people were less Catholic than members of religious communities. The goal of the university leadership was better described as declericalization than secularization.

This point was made in a very interesting memo to Fordham's board of trustees in July 1968 from Rev. Edmund G. Ryan, S.J., when the addition of laymen to the board was being discussed. As described in chapter 2, anxiety about the forthcoming Gellhorn report coupled with the concern over eligibility for the Bundy grants placed this question foremost on the Fordham trustees' agenda. Father Ryan discussed the different meanings of "secularization," pointing to the equivocal usage of the term by alumni in their letters denouncing the administration and also by the administrators themselves, who used imprecise language open to misinterpretation. Citing the McGrath report as having undercut the notion that the Society of Jesus owned Fordham, Ryan argued that "the fact that the present trustees are all Jesuits does not vest the ownership in the Society of Jesus." Consequently, he went on, adding laymen to the board does not secularize the university.

"Since the property wasn't Church or religious property initially, a change in the composition of the Board in no way changes the ownership." He also cited the Land O'Lakes statement with approval, arguing that Fordham's adherence to that statement precluded adoption of a form of secularism that would exclude God from human life. Alumni have equated "declericalization" with "secularization," thus seeing Fordham on the road to an abandonment of religious principles. Ryan, like McGrath, emphasized the positive contribution that the sponsoring body could make to the life of the university. He defended Fordham's "Christian secularity" and saw state funding as consonant with being a Catholic university.[30]

The reliance on McGrath's canonical opinion and the movement toward independent boards among the Catholic colleges and universities in the United States did not go unnoticed in Rome. Although both the University of Notre Dame and Saint Louis University had carried on extensive conversation with authorities in Rome prior to their decisions, many other Catholic colleges simply assumed that there was no need for an indult of alienation when they organized new boards and structured new relationships between the colleges and the religious communities. They may well have thought that if Notre Dame and Saint Louis could do it, there was no problem. Congregations without Roman headquarters—which included many Sisters' groups—believed that a decision of their General Council was all that was needed, especially if the property (according to McGrath) had never really belonged to the religious community. Very few expressed concern about the prescriptions of the canon law in this regard.[31]

But the view from the Vatican was somewhat different. Alarmed by reports from the United States that religious communities were "turning over" their colleges and universities to groups of laymen, the Secretary of the Congregation for Catholic Education, Gabriel Marie Cardinal Garrone, sent Archbishop Jean Jadot, the Apostolic Delegate in Washington, a draft of a letter in January 1974 which he and the Secretary of the Congregation for Religious intended to send the American bishops and the organizations of major superiors, known as the Leadership Conference of Women Religious (LCWR) and the Conference of Major Superiors of Men (CMSM). In the letter Garrone denounced the McGrath thesis as unacceptable and asked for a report on the "exact civil and canonical status" of all institutions that call themselves "Catholic." The tone of the letter was highly accusatory, stating that the "alienations" of property were probably "invalid both canonically and civilly."[32] Apparently, Jadot had a moderating influence on the Cardinal, for the letter that was actually sent on October 7, 1974 to John Cardinal Krol, president of the National Conference of Catholic Bishops, for distribution to the American bishops expressed concern about the confusion being caused about the "Catholic character" of the institutions and asked that a joint commission of NCCB, CMSM, and LCWR be set up to study the situation. "We believe it necessary, first of all, to know which institutions, at the present moment, are or consider themselves Catholic." In the meantime, the two Roman Congregations wished the commission to ask the universities not to make further changes until the situation was reviewed. It was made clear that the McGrath thesis had never been accepted as valid.[33]

In response to this letter, the NCCB Committee on Law and Public Policy considered the McGrath thesis at its meeting in December 1974. It found that the thesis had "achieved acceptance far beyond its merits" and recommended that a comprehensive and detailed study be undertaken. In the opinion of the committee, the issue was urgent because the McGrath thesis was gaining currency and irreparable harm might result to the interests of the church. McGrath's thesis "regarding secular control over the operations and property of the incorporated Catholic institutions and agencies has vast implications for the autonomy, witness, and mission of the Church in America."[34]

Accordingly, the committee set up a Commission on Ownership of Catholic Institutions to study the question in depth. At what turned out to be its only meeting, on January 24, 1975, the commission heard a report from Rev. Michael Sheehan, assistant general secretary for NCCB.[35] Sheehan summarized the McGrath thesis, explained the counterarguments of Rev. Adam Maida, a canonist who defended church property rights, and reported on the opinions of a group of attorneys who had been asked to review the legal issues involved. The joint commission then made three recommendations to the NCCB Administrative Committee: (1) NCCB should commission a comprehensive study on the ownership and control of Church property in the U.S.A.; (2) Interim guidelines should be prepared by the General Counsel of the United States Catholic Conference (USCC, the administrative arm of the NCCB) concerning the corporate structure of Catholic institutions, their relationship to the sponsoring religious congregations, and the vital questions of ownership and control; and (3) Efforts to collect information as to the Catholic character of the institutions at this time would be counterproductive and should be deferred until after the study was made.

These recommendations were forwarded to Rome on March 6, 1975 by Archbishop Bernardin, then president of NCCB, with the comment that the newly published work by Rev. Adam Maida was being sent to each of the bishops and could provide interim guidelines.[36] In this same letter, Archbishop Bernardin asked for clarification about the roles of the joint NCCB/LCWR/CMSM commission and that of an existing committee set up in December 1974 under the leadership of Bishop William Borders and the College and University Department of NCEA and known as the bishops and presidents' committee.[37]

The *raison d'être* for the bishops and presidents' committee was a letter to the episcopal conferences from Cardinal Garrone on April 10, 1974, requesting a follow-up on the document issued in 1972, *The Catholic University in the Modern World*. Although that document, drawn up by delegates to a conference in Rome, had been approved by the Congregation for Catholic Education and Pope Paul VI, Garrone had attached a caveat to the effect that there were still unresolved questions about the relationship of the universities to the church. Now, in 1974, he wished the bishops to reflect upon the implementation of the document and to set up a committee "to handle Catholic university problems."[38]

Confusion had resulted from the fact that while the bishops and presidents' committee understood itself as the forum for discussing the "Catholic university problems" noted by Garrone, the joint commission (NCCB/LCWR/CMSM) to study the problems connected with possible "alienation" of property by hospitals or universities through changing governance structures had been established without any notification to Bishop Borders, as chair of the bishops and presidents' committee, or to the executive director of the College and University Department of NCEA. If, as Cardinal Garrone suggested, the property question was connected to the Catholic identity of the institutions, ought not representatives of the committee charged by the Holy See with "discussing Catholic university problems" be participants in the work of this new commission?

As a result of protests from Archbishop Borders and Msgr. John F. Murphy, executive director of the College and University Department, Archbishop May, chair of the joint commission, invited Murphy to participate in the work of the commission. The latter so informed the legal counsel at NCCB/USCC, Mr. Eugene Krasicky, but no subsequent meetings of the commission were ever held. The correspondence from then on between Krasicky and Murphy deals with the recommendation of the committee for a thorough study of the questions by expert legal advisors. By the end of 1975, when no meeting of the commission had been scheduled and no progress made on having a study done by USCC, the bishops and presidents' committee at its meeting of December 14 encouraged Msgr. Murphy to set up an *ad hoc* committee to study the questions. He immediately invited Rev. Frederick R. McManus of the Canon Law faculty at The Catholic University of America to assist him in setting up such a committee.[39] The work of the resulting Committee on Property of Colleges and Universities (COPCU) produced position papers that were then discussed in regional meetings under the auspices of the College and University Department of NCEA.

This project coincided with the 1977 establishment of the ecumenically-sponsored Center for Constitutional Studies at the University of Notre Dame, under the leadership of Rev. James Burtchaell, C.S.C., and the direction of Mr. Philip Moots. Within a few years, two important monographs which dealt with church-related higher education in the United States had been published: *The Church and Campus* and *The Government and Campus*.[40] These works were helpful in sorting through the legal implications of "church" ownership in the American legal context. However, the debate about the propriety, and even canonical validity, of the transfer of an institution and/or property used by it from control by a religious community to a board of trustees that was independent of the community continues today in Catholic higher education circles.[41]

During the next few decades, the public image of Catholic higher education changed dramatically. To the broader world outside its own campuses, its "independence" of church control was taken for granted. The predominance of lay persons in both administration and governance of the colleges and universities rendered academic the discussions about the canon law status of laity. The leadership of the institutions were free to compete with their colleagues in other private universities for funding and academic prestige. Legally, the Catholic colleges had demonstrated their freedom from ecclesial authority. After the *Tilton* decision of 1971, the question of their eligibility for government funding seemed settled in their favor, provided they were careful not to appear "sectarian."

At the same time, the changes made in the governance of the colleges created some new problems: a lessening of interest on the part of some religious in the mission of Catholic higher education; a loss of a distinctive Catholic culture on many campuses; and perhaps most understandably, an ambiguity about the mission itself.

Conclusion

The actions taken in the seven institutions studied here were followed by similar decisions on the part of
most Catholic colleges and universities in the decade that
followed. As Stamm pointed out, by 1977 independence in
governance characterized the majority of institutions in
his study. This revolution was accomplished in a variety
of ways: a revision of bylaws, the addition of lay persons
to already existing boards of trustees, and/or the separate
incorporation of religious communities or colleges where
needed. The accountability of the president to the board
was now an accomplished fact. Even where power to alienate property was reserved to "corporate" Members who
were exclusively religious, it was no longer in virtue of the
religious authority of the house or provincial council that
their decisions concerning the administration of the college
were made, but in virtue of their legal status as Members of
a corporation.

As we have seen, the officials at the Congregation of
Catholic Education at the Vatican expressed concern in
1974 about this transfer of governing authority, particularly
as it affected the canonical status of the properties.[1] Rome
also raised the question of the continued "Catholicity" of
institutions where control had been handed over to lay persons. It would take us too far afield to discuss this Roman
initiative in detail, but it is important to note that in raising
the question of the "Catholic" identity of the institutions
once the property was transferred to lay control, the Holy
See revealed certain presuppositions. One assumption in

the 1974 letter was that the definition of the "Catholicity" of an institution depended on being controlled by a religious community. Another assumption, despite the Congregation's knowledge that transfers had taken place during the 1960s, was that a bishop or a major superior was still "responsible" for the institution.

For the next twenty years these questions would be debated by delegates of Catholic universities around the world with bishops and the Congregation of Catholic Education. They would come into dramatic focus in the discussions prior to the promulgation of the Code of Canon Law in 1983, and would persist in the dialogue which preceded and followed the Apostolic Constitution, *Ex Corde Ecclesiae,* issued August 15, 1990.[2]

The founding religious communities of the American Catholic colleges and universities, as we have seen, had moved to a new partnership with lay leaders. This was done in response to several factors, some internal to the church and the religious orders, and others in response to the culture of the external academic community. The shift in control had occurred in different ways on different campuses and had taken shape according to the particular history of each institution and the vision of its leaders. A detailed study of each individual institution is needed in order to ascertain the reasons that predominated in that specific instance, but our seven case studies indicate common objectives that we could expect to find elsewhere.

In summary, I would suggest that the purposes for which governing boards of Catholic colleges and universities were reorganized so as to bring laymen into the power stucture were many and complex: (1) to achieve that level of educational excellence which would allow them to compete in the academic world with other private universities; (2) to gather the needed resources to support this step upward by more efficacious use of the expertise of lay advisory boards in the areas of finance and management; (3) to change the image of the university in the eyes of local communities, state and federal granting agencies, and the national higher education community, moving away from the common perception that they were "run" by the Catholic church and thus constituted a sub-culture; (4) to secure strong lay participation in fund-raising efforts through alumni/ae and trustee contacts with foundations and corporations; (5) to bring a more realistic understanding of the secular world to the decision-making process as lay persons assisted the college administrators in their dealings with lay faculty and students.

While the shift in ecclesiology concerning the role of the laity which appeared in the documents of Vatican II was a strong supporting argument for the development of the new partnership, it was not a major cause of it. It became an important talking point for presidents as they sought to convey the new reality to alumni/ae, members of their religious communities, potential lay trustees, and American and Roman church authorities. A strong commitment on the part of all these groups to the future of the institutions rendered moot the canonical question as to the "Catholicity" of the university. Apart from the church authorities, these participants had never linked the ownership of the property by the religious community to the institution's degree of Catholicity. From their point of view, the university would now be held in trust by an independent board composed of lay and religious members, but the change would not alter its identity as a Catholic institution.

Thus, the issues raised by Cardinal Garrone in 1974 were answered more by historical evolution than by canonical scholarship. Already in their responses to Garrone in 1974, the colleges reported that they had implemented the document *The Catholic University in the Modern World* more by the stress they placed on "Christian living" than on theories about the role of the university or the criteria for its "Catholicity" as spelled out in the document.[3] The theological and canonical ambiguities surfaced only when clarity was sought by the Congregation for Catholic Education or by an individual bishop who had to face teaching or behavior which he considered inconsistent with the university's character as Catholic.

Finally, a clear conclusion of this study is that in each case the key figure in the change of governance was the president, typically a member of the religious community which founded the college. In the years under review there was an extraordinarily gifted cohort of men and women in that office. Inspired by the ecclesial climate fostered by John XXIII and Vatican Council II, the presidents built on the spirit of ecumenism, individual freedom of conscience, and a positive theology of the world which fostered greater collaboration with their counterparts in secular universities. To their credit, they were able to inspire significant lay persons to assume roles of responsibility in these Catholic institutions. With well-placed trustees able to open doors to foundations and corporations and with religious superiors willing to guard them from serious internal dissonance, the presidents were empowered to move forward. With legal counsel strongly influenced by the *Horace Mann* case and with an interesting lack of concern about canonical issues which led them to accept the McGrath thesis quite uncritically, these presidents were highly successful in achieving their goals.

Catholic institutions of higher education would have serious financial crises to deal with in the seventies, but now they would be able to identify themselves with other "independent" colleges and universities, a possiblity that enabled their students to share equitably in the grants and loans that were authorized in the Higher Education Acts of 1965 and 1972. While they still had a long way to go to achieve the kind of academic reputation they desired, they now had far greater resources and, even more importantly, they had control over them. The lay trustees who became the governors of the university were handpicked by the presidents, and since the new boards were self-perpetuating, this created a strong support group for the president and gave continuity to the plans of the university.

In the specific institutions that we have studied, religious superiors fully supported the presidents in their move toward greater lay participation in governance. Even at Saint Michael's College and Fordham University, where the forced resignations of the presidents occurred during this transition, the causes for the resignations had other roots. But there were colleges where such enthusiastic support was not forthcoming from community leadership. In some instances, efforts were made to retain control through various mechanisms. In other situations, the religious community saw an opportunity to withdraw its support from the college in order to pursue other priorities in its apostolic work. The attitude of apostolic detachment expressed by the Holy Cross provincial in his letter to the province in 1966 (which we have cited in chapter 2) was not universally shared, and it was to be a long struggle (still going on) to discover how to walk the path of influence when there was no longer control.

Having studied the changes, the reasons for those changes, and the processes followed in making them, it seems clear that in the late sixties Catholic colleges and universities took a major step in the aculturation process that

Gleason has described. Without the decisions made at that time, it is unlikely that Catholic colleges and universities in the United States would be as highly respected by their peers in higher education as many of them are, and would have the resources to continue their mission of education in their own distinctive tradition. If the leaders today can hand on that tradition to the trustees of their institutions, then the future will be one of lasting influence, an influence that survives beyond the relinquishment of control.

Archives

AAJCU   Archives, Association of Jesuit Colleges and Universities

ACHC   Archives, College of the Holy Cross

ACNR   Archives, College of New Rochelle

ACST   Archives, Convent of St. Teresa

ACUA-NCEA   Archives, The Catholic University of America, National Catholic Educational Association Collection. This includes the records of the Association of Catholic Colleges and Universities, referred to between 1904 and 1978 as the College and University Department of NCEA.

AFU   Archives, Fordham University

AIPHC   Archives, Indiana Province of the Congregation of Holy Cross

AMC   Archives, Mundelein College

AMPSJ   Archives, Missouri Province of the Society of Jesus

ANCCB   Archives, National Conference of Catholic Bishops

ANYSJ   Archives, New York Province Society of Jesus

ASLU   Archives, Saint Louis University

ASMC   Archives, Saint Michael's College

ASSE   Archives, Society of St. Edmund

AUND   Archives, University of Notre Dame

AUPE   Archives, Ursuline Provincialate Eastern Province

Notes

Preface

1. This number is from Charles E. Ford and Edgar L. Roy, *The Renewal of Catholic Higher Education* (Washington, D.C.: NCEA, 1968). Other studies give other numbers, depending on what is included and excluded, e.g., seminaries. I have also used the work of Earl J. McGrath and Gerald E. Dupont, *The Future Governance of Catholic Higher Education in the United States*, 1967, and the New York State Advisory Committee on Educational Leadership, *College and University Trustees and Trusteeship*, 1966. The various publications of Rev. Andrew Greeley also contain statistics on Catholic higher education as well as insightful comments of interpretation; see especially *From Backwater to Mainstream* (New York: McGraw-Hill, 1969).

2. This expression was used by Rev. Avery Dulles, S.J. (*The New York Times*, May 1, 1991), but the concept behind it had been developed by James Tunstead Burtchaell, C.S.C., "The Decline and Fall of the Christian College," *First Things*, parts 1 (April 1991, pp. 16–29) and 2 (May 1991, pp. 20–38).

3. Philip J. Gleason, *Contending With Modernity: Catholic Higher Education in the Twentieth Century* (New York: Oxford University Press, 1995).

4. Philip J. Gleason, *What Made Catholic Identity a Problem?* Marianist Award Lecture, University of Dayton, 1994.

5. John McGrath's published work appeared in 1968 as *Catholic Institutions in the United States: Canonical and Civil Law Status* (Washington, D.C.: The Catholic University of America Press, 1968). However, from 1965 to 1968 he was a popular visitor to campuses and gave oral presentations on the subject.

1. Separation: The Purpose and the Pain

1. This comment was made at the three-day meeting at Notre Dame in September 1992, when Father Theodore Hesburgh, C.S.C., Father Paul Reinert, S.J., Sister Ann Ida Gannon, B.V.M., Edmund Stephan, and Daniel Schlafly met with the author to reflect on the changes made in 1967. Tapes of this meeting are in possession of the author.

2. Ford and Roy, *The Renewal of Catholic Higher Education.* Although published in 1968, the report was based on data from a 1964–65 survey.

3. Ibid., p. 17.

4. Rev. Paul Reinert, S.J., "Toward Renewal: The Development of Catholic Higher Education," NCEA Convention, March 29, 1967; ACUA-NCEA.

5. John Tracy Ellis, "American Catholics and the Intellectual Life," *Thought* 30 (Autumn 1955). His ideas were already well known even before publication of this article, since he had articulated them on many college campuses and had presented drafts of his paper at two meetings of the Catholic Commission on Intellectual and Cultural Affairs (CCICA).

6. Neil J. McClusky, S.J., "The New Catholic College," *America* (March 25, 1967): 414–17.

7. Andrew Greeley, "Laicization of Catholic Colleges," *Christian Century* (March 12, 1967).

8. See, for example, the pastoral letter of Archbishop Joseph E. Ritter of Saint Louis, June 17, 1960, in which he forcefully reminds parents that they must seek his permission, through their pastors, if they find it necessary to send their children to secular or non-Catholic colleges. "Parents and students have . . . the grave responsibility of choosing Catholic colleges where the atmosphere and the teaching are conducive to the proper end of Christian education"; ACUA-NCEA.

9. Minutes of the Council, Convent of Saint Teresa, New Rochelle, New York, October 23, 1958, ACST.

10. Jay P. Dolan, *The American Catholic Experience* (Garden City, N.J.: Doubleday and Co., 1985), pp. 436–38.

11. J. McGrath, *Catholic Institutions: Canonical and Civil Law Status*. See preface, note 5.

12. Martin J. Stamm, "Emerging Models of Governance in Contemporary American Catholic Higher Education," *Current Issues in Catholic Higher Education*, vol. 2, no. 1 (Summer 1981):43. This article is based on Stamm's doctoral dissertation on the laicization of boards, done at the University of Pennsylvania, 1979. The prevailing models of unicameral and bicameral governance are discussed in chapter 3.

13. These reflections were shared with the author at the Notre Dame meeting in September 1992; see note 1 above. This personal element has richly supplemented the documentary evidence contained in archives.

14. Ibid.

15. The Association of Catholic Colleges and Universities had been founded in 1899. In 1904 it had merged with the Association of Parish Schools and the Association of Seminaries to form the National Catholic Educational Association. Its designation underwent several changes, but in the period we are considering it was known as the College and University Department of NCEA. In 1978 it resumed its original name and is now known as the Association of Catholic Colleges and Universities.

16. For the gradual shift in AAC's thinking, see discussions in the *Bulletin* of the Association from 1958 to 1970.

17. Paul A. Fitzgerald, S.J., *The Governance of Jesuit Colleges in the United States, 1920–1970* (Notre Dame, Ind.: University of Notre Dame Press, 1984), chapters 7–12. The AJCU was founded in the summer of 1970 with a board of directors composed of the presidents of the twenty-eight institutions.

18. See, for example, the letters of Gerald Dupont to many of the other persons named; ASMC, Dupont papers. The writings and opinions of Charles Wilson, James O'Connor, S.J., and Charles Horgan are also found in the archives of the various

institutions. Their importance as legal counsel will be referred to in chapters 2 and 3.

19. "Functions of Boards of Trustees in Higher Education," *AGB REPORTS* vol. 7, no. 5 (June 1965); a reprint of the Middle States document.

20. New York State Advisory Committee on Educational Leadership, *College and University Trustees and Trusteeship*, 1966.

21. Manning M. Pattillo Jr. and Donald M. Mackenzie, *Eight Hundred Colleges Face the Future: A Preliminary Report* (St Louis: The Danforth Foundation, 1965).

22. Alcuin W. Tasch, "Organization and Statutes," in *College Organization and Administration*, ed. Roy Deferrari (Washington, D.C., The Catholic University of America Press, 1947), pp. 61–64.

23. Ibid.

24. Ibid., p. 63.

25. Edward Stanford, O.S.A., *A Guide to Catholic College Administration* (Westminster, Md.: The Newman Press, 1965). His book was based not only on his experience as president of Villanova University but even more, perhaps, on what he had learned as one of three full-time consultants at AAC on governance and administration. He visited over 140 Catholic campuses and reported on them in his book. In his visits he often had the opportunity of speaking with trustees as well as administrators and faculty, and he gained a certain stature as a visiting expert. There are references to his visits at the College of New Rochelle to consult with Charles Horgan, legal counsel. At Mundelein College, Sister Ann Ida thought so highly of his ideas that she gave a copy of his book to all of her trustees for Christmas 1965. Both Father Stanford and his book seem to have been quite influential on Catholic campuses.

26. Ibid., p. 15.

27. Ford and Roy, *The Renewal of Catholic Higher Education*, p. 7.

28. E. McGrath and Dupont, *The Future Governance of Catholic Higher Education in the United States*. Although there is no

publisher given, the study was done under the auspices of the Institute of Higher Education at Columbia University of which Dr. McGrath was the director.

29. Ibid., p. 13.

30. *Horace Mann League v Board of Public Works of Maryland*, 242 Md. 645, 220 A2d 51, cert denied, appeal dismissed 385 US 97 (1966). For a full discussion of this case, see chapter 3.

31. Annals, October 1958, ACST.

2. Independence: The Process of Laicization

1. The materials on which this section is based are in the archives of the College of New Rochelle (ACNR), the Community of St. Teresa (ACST), and the Eastern Province USA of the Roman Union of Ursulines (AUPE). Most of the information comes from the minutes of the board of trustees and its Executive Committee and the local and provincial council minutes. Surprisingly, little correspondence on these matters survives. The convent corporation referred to is that of the local community and is called St. Teresa.

2. Minutes of the board of trustees, ACNR.

3. Cf. James T. Schleifer, *The College of New Rochelle* (Virginia Beach, Va.: Donning Company, 1994).

4. In 1956–57 an unfortunate conflict between four priests in the Religion Department and four lay faculty in Philosophy and English had strained relations on campus, though there was little public knowledge of what was going on behind the scenes. Through the mediation of Cardinal Spellman, the situation was finally resolved, but by then lay faculty had become interested in AAUP and had proposed a committee on tenure and a faculty handbook that would spell out their rights. Much of this was achieved by 1964.

5. For several years the long-range plan of the college had included a "faculty residence" for the nuns of the community. By 1969 both trustees and community agreed that for legal reasons it would be best to have the nuns finance their own new convent,

and property exchanges were carried out to enable them to do so. The main building, the "Castle," which was the residence for the nuns who did not live with the students, and the summer home which had been given to the nuns by a benefactor were now returned to the nuns, having been ceded to the college corporation in 1958. Gifts from alumnae and other friends which had been given for the faculty residence were also turned over to the convent corporation.

6. The law firm in which Mr. Horgan practiced was that of Muldoon and Horgan. Both Mr. Muldoon and Mr. Horgan served as legal counsel and attended New Rochelle trustee meetings as trustees. In 1967 Mr. Horgan resigned as trustee to avoid a conflict with his role as legal counsel to the college. He was also legal counsel to the Community of St. Teresa and to the Eastern Province, which simplified much of the reorganization. However in 1970, in order to deal with the agreement about property, the Convent of St. Teresa hired a different legal counsel. Horgan remained as counsel to New Rochelle until his death in 1979.

7. Correspondence between Horgan and Raymond Swords, S.J., and George W. Nolan, S.J., 1967, ACHC.

8. Details are given in chapter 3.

9. Memo from Ewald Nyquist to the president of New Rochelle, February 19, 1970; College of New Rochelle Bundy files at Cusack and Stiles, New York City.

10. Convocation Address, November 21, 1966, in Jacqueline Grennan, *Where I am Going* (New York: McGraw Hill, 1968). Other addresses in this collection are instructive in tracing the development of Grennan's thought. An interesting contrast can be made with her address to the Peace Corps in Washington, D.C., in March 1965 where she said: "I would like to say that I come to you as a person who, at I hope young middle age, lives within a complex of rigid institutions, one called a religious order, one called the Roman Catholic Church, one called the establishment of higher education. I live within it lyrically at age thirty-eight, with my eyes wide open, saying that I want only to be a *worldly* nun, because the world is the only place in which I can operate."

Evidently by the end of 1966 she had decided that she could no longer live within the "complex of rigid institutions."

11. See Jacqueline Grennan, "Freeing the Catholic College from Juridical Control by the Church," *Journal of Higher Education* (February 1969): 101–107.

12. This section is based on materials in the archives of Saint Louis University (ASLU) and in the provincial archives of the Missouri Province of the Society of Jesus (AMPSJ). In addition to minutes of the trustees and of the provincial council, the archives include correspondence between university officials and the provincial and also with the Father General, Father Arrupe at the time.

13. News release from Saint Louis University, January 21, 1967, ASLU.

14. *The Constitution, History, and Charter of Saint Louis University*, Saint Louis, Missouri, 1964. See articles I and IV.

15. Ibid., article V.

16. See chapter 3 for a discussion of Father O'Connor's position paper on the question.

17. Confidential memo from Paul Reinert to trustees on the Executive Committee of Saint Louis, March 21, 1966, ASLU.

18. Ibid., p. 2.

19. E. J. Drummond, memo to Executive Committee, April 13, 1966, ASLU Bylaws file. Walter Ong, S.J., an outstanding scholar, was well known as an author and lecturer on the subject of the intellectual apostolate. See, for example, his *American Catholic Crossroads* (New York: MacMillan, 1959).

20. Rev. Trafford P. Maher, S.J., to Paul C. Reinert, S.J., June 27, 1966, ASLU Bylaws file.

21. Robert Henle, S.J., memo to the board, April 15, 1966, ASLU. Father Henle was academic vice president at Saint Louis and dean of the Graduate School. He later became president of Georgetown. In an interview with him on January 7, 1993, I learned of several factors that influenced his thinking: the growth of Saint Louis University; the need for the university to be recognized by American higher education circles; the dual role of the

rector-president; and the ambiguous position of the superior's consultors with reference to the decisions of the university.

22. Arrupe to Thro, October 30, 1966, AMPSJ.

23. Reinert to Schlafly, December 28, 1966, ASLU Bylaws file.

24. ASLU Bylaws file.

25. Thomas V. Connelly to Jerome J. Marchetti, S.J., December 16, 1966 and January 3, 1967; ASLU Bylaws file.

26. Bylaws of Saint Louis University, 1967, adopted March 15, 1967.

27. See note 16.

28. Memo from Paul Reinert to the participants of Meeting of Presidents and Representatives of Jesuit Colleges and Universities at Saint Louis University, May 20–21, 1967, ASLU. The minutes, including Reinert's summary, were not transcribed from tapes and distributed until a year later. In the intervening year, many of the other Jesuit colleges had begun to develop their own reorganization plans, and McGrath's work had also been published.

29. "Foundation Statements and Articles Relevant to the Jesuit Community at Saint Louis University," signed by Gerald R. Sheahan, S.J., provincial of the Missouri Province; William V. Stauder, S.J., rector of the Jesuit Community at Saint Louis University; and Paul C. Reinert, S.J., president of Saint Louis University, September 1, 1967; AMPSJ.

30. Unlike most presidents of Catholic colleges at the time, Reinert had taken his doctorate at the University of Chicago in higher education administration. He recalled at the meeting held in 1992 that he was astonished and even appalled at the way in which Saint Louis was run compared to the canons of higher education administration which he had studied. He arrived in the Saint Louis dean's office in 1944 and became president in 1949. He knew the world of secular higher education, and in the years that followed became a respected player in it; clearly he was not about to tolerate the kind of oversight being exercised by the religious community. Through his leadership in the College and University Department of NCEA and his presence in AAC and on the various commissions that studied the condition of higher

education throughout the 1960s and 1970s, he exerted enormous influence. In the reorganization of the Jesuit Educational Association and the establishment of the Association of Jesuit Colleges and Universities, he was a major force. In addition, he was known by many presidents and deans in Catholic women's colleges and other small institutions as a person to whom one could go for information and advice. Even his critics respected him for his integrity and courage.

31. Letter from Arrupe to Sponga, November 27, 1967, quoted in a memo of Father Reinert. The presidents' responses are also contained in this memo, which was given by Father Reinert to the author. No date is given for the submission of the responses to Father General.

32. Arrupe was evidently delaying further movement toward lay boards until some of his questions were answered. Both Holy Cross and Georgetown had requested permission to move ahead but for several months had heard nothing. In a letter of Raymond J. Swords, S.J., president of Holy Cross, to Charles Horgan, August 1, 1967, Swords referred to Father Campbell's equal frustration at Georgetown and commented that it was possible that "someone has written and thrown a few roadblocks." Campbell had spoken in exasperation of the fact that many women's colleges were already doing what they lacked courage to do; ACHC, Swords papers.

33. In 1963, for example, both Fordham and Saint Louis were upset at a decree from Rome that all honorary degrees must be approved by the Sacred Congregation. At the NCEA meeting in 1964 a resolution was passed to request that this be withdrawn. Word came through the good offices of Cardinal Spellman that the Apostolic Delegate had explained the impossibility of such "control" being exerted over Catholic colleges in the United States. Interview with Rev. Vincent O'Keefe, president of Fordham; Cicognani to Spellman, March 24, 1964, AFU.

34. Fitzgerald, *Governance of Jesuit Colleges*, p. 205.

35. The basis for this section is the archival collection at the University of Notre Dame (AUND), including the Hesburgh

Papers, the materials relative to the development of the lay board, and the papers relating to the International Federation of Catholic Universities. In addition, the provincial archives of the Indiana Province of the Congregation of Holy Cross (AIPHC) have the complete records of the chapters and the correspondence with Rome concerning Notre Dame and Portland. Relevant files in the university archives are: UPHS, PPHS, UDIS, CPHS, UBLT, UBTS, CMCA, UBTR.

36. For the various documents see Gallin, *American Catholic Higher Education: Essential Documents, 1967–1990* (Notre Dame, Ind.: University of Notre Dame Press, 1992).

37. In March 1966 Hesburgh presented figures that demonstrated growth, and which he used as a major argument for his position:

	1945	1965
Students	3300	7000
Faculty	260	530
Faculty salaries	750,000	8,900,000
Operating budget	4,000,000	28,000,000
Endowment	5,000,000	56,000,000
Buildings	10,000,000	57,000,000

Report to Steering Committee of the Lay Trustees Development Committee, March 13–15, 1966; and minutes of the meeting June 23–25; AUND, UBLT Box 2.

38. Hesburgh to Lalande, November 4, 1966, AUND.

39. Howard J. Kenna, C.S.C., to the Priests of the Holy Cross, Indiana Province, December 13, 1966, AIPHC.

40. Andrew Greeley, "The Catholic Campus," *The Critic* (October–November 1966), quoted in Howard Kenna's letter to the province, December 13, 1966, AIPHC.

41. David Riesman and Christopher Jencks, "The Viability of the American College," in Nevitt Sanford, *The American College* (New York; Wiley and Son, 1962), p. 91.

42. Hesburgh speech to chapter, January 25, 1967, AUND.

43. Rev. John Walsh, C.S.C., "Regional Report for North America," paper delivered at the IFCU Assembly in Kinshasa, Zaire, September 1968; AUND, ICFU file.

44. Bernard Mullahy to Kenna, May 27, 1966, AIPHC.

45. Lalande to Hesburgh, January 27, 1964, AUND.

46. Letter from Hesburgh to the faculty at Notre Dame from Pucon, Chile, February 23, 1967, AUND; also used as introduction to the 1967 Faculty Manual. These same images of a beacon and a bridge are found in a "position paper" presumably prepared for the Holy Cross chapter, AUND.

47. All of the materials for this section come from the archives of Mundelein College (AMC), now a part of Loyola University of Chicago. Sister Ann Ida is the current archivist and has been extremely helpful to the author by supplying the relevant documents.

48. *Mundelein College Report*, February/March 1967, p. 4, AMC.

49. Faculty Meeting Minutes, February 7, 1967, AMC.

50. *Mundelein College Report*, August/September 1967, AMC.

51. Minutes of an executive session of the Members, December 27, 1967, AMC.

52. Talk delivered to chapter on January 24, 1967 by Rev. Paul E. Waldschmidt, C.S.C.; AIPHC.

53. Letter of Waldschmidt to Kenna, June 19, 1966, AIPHC.

54. The material used in reconstructing the events at Saint Michael's is found in Gerald Dupont's file in the college archives (ASMC) and in the Society of St. Edmund archives (ASSE).

55. Father Gerald Dupont, S.S.E., was a member of the network which facilitated conversations among the presidents interested in moving to independent boards. He was one of the organizers of a series of seminars on Catholic college administration held at The Catholic University of America in the 1950s and 1960s under the leadership of Roy Deferrari. He coauthored a study of trusteeship with Earl McGrath and had extensive contacts with him and with Stanford. He attended the workshop at Loretto Heights held on February 9 and 10, 1968, where he shared

ideas with the other participants such as Paul Reinert, John Mc-Grath, Jacqueline Grennan and Edmund Stephan. It was not surprising, therefore, that he introduced the notion of a more broadly-based trusteeship at Saint Michael's.

56. Quoted by Dupont from Stanford's *Guide to Catholic College Administration*, p. 13; ASMC.

57. Dupont to Galligan, July 11, 1968; Galligan to Dupont, August 29, 1968, in which reference is made to conversations of June 3 and July 6 and to Dupont's letters of July 11 and August 1; ASMC.

58. Galligan to Dupont, August 29, 1968, ASMC. A first draft of the letter, in the files of the Society of St. Edmund, has even more explicit comments (ASSE).

59. Although the draft of September 1, 1968 is contained in the Board of Trustees Meeting file, the approved agreement seems to be the one of 1970: "Agreement between The Society of Saint Edmund and Saint Michael's College," September 11, 1970, and amendment of October 4, 1987; ASMC. The earlier draft contains much more by way of rationale for the proposed agreement.

60. Dupont to Galligan, September 6, 1968, ASMC.

61. The announcement appeared in the lcoal newspaper, the *Daily Herald,* September 14, 1968.

62. Information on Fordham was gained from documents in both the archives of the New York Province, Society of Jesus (ANYSJ), and of Fordham University (AFU). The talk given by McLaughlin to the Jesuit presidents is found in *Proceedings* of the Jesuit Educational Association, June 27, 1967.

63. Father Laurence McGinley was another long-time leader in Catholic higher education and a member of the presidents' network which we have described. In virtue of the various experiments regarding rector/president/superior roles noted above, he managed to remain in office as president from 1949 to 1963. A contemporary of Reinert and Hesburgh, he too was known on the state and national levels of higher education. He was a member of the Middle States Association Commission and

served on the New York State task force headed by Dr. Perkins which studied trusteeship and released its report in 1967. He was also a close friend of Ewald (Joe) Nyquist, chair of the Middle States Commission in the late 1950s and early 1960s before going to Albany as Commissioner of Higher Education. McGinley was recognized among the colleges in New York State for his important work with both the public and private sectors of higher education. His bold new ventures in coeducation and in creating Fordham at Lincoln Center placed him in the forefront of Catholic higher education.

64. McLaughlin, Inaugural Address, October 18, 1965, AFU.

65. McLaughlin, President's Report 1965–1967, AFU.

66. Arrupe, Convocation Address, in *The University in the American Experience* (New York: Fordham University Press, 1966).

67. McLaughlin, in a speech given at the AGB Convention, April 17, 1967; published in 1967 *AGB Reports*.

68. Royall, Koegel, Rogers, and Wells, letter to McLaughlin, November 15, 1967, AFU.

69. Quoted from the introduction of the final report by Walter Gellhorn and R. Kent Greenawalt, "An Independent Fordham, A Choice for Catholic Higher Education," October 1968; AFU.

70. John J. Meng to Walter Gelhorn, July 26, 1968; AFU, PM63.

71. Rev. Robert Drinan, S.J., was at that time dean of the Boston College Law School and a lecturer of note on questions of civil rights and political action.

72. See chapter 1 on the McGrath-Dupont study.

73. The terminology used here, "free Christian college," comes from the Danforth study on church-related higher education. See chapter 1, note 21.

74. "Official Statement of the Board of Trustees of Fordham University," October 30, 1968; AFU, PM63.

75. McLaughlin to Gellhorn, September 25, 1968, AFU.

76. Memo from Edwin A. Quain, S.J., to Dr. Arthur Brown and Mr. Robert Kidera, October 31, 1968, AFU. Mr. Kidera was

Vice President for University Relations and had evidently requested the printing.

77. McLaughlin was appointed chancellor, but both he and his executive vice president left Fordham within the year.

78. The changes are summarized in a memo of January 27, 1969, provided by Kidera to Walsh, the new president, at Walsh's request. Walsh had asked Kidera for a list of the recommendations that had been made in the Gellhorn report and a report of which ones had been or were being implemented. In all, the memo lists sixteen recommendations, each with a "status" report; AFU.

79. President's Report 1968–69, AFU.

80. An account of the meeting and the argument made there was given to the author in an interview on June 14, 1995 by President Paul Reiss at Saint Michael's College. Mr. Reiss was academic vice president at Fordham and participated in the meeting with Dr. Nyquist and Mr. Stone.

3. Legal Concerns

1. J. McGrath, *Catholic Institutions: Canonical and Civil Law Status.* In the foreword, McGrath notes that the basic research in canon law was done by one of his students, Rev. John J. Zemanick, S.S.E. He was from Saint Michael's College and Father Dupont, president at the time, seems to have been instrumental in getting him to study canon law with McGrath. In the light of Father Robert Kennedy's critique of McGrath, one wonders if the basic research may have suffered from this delegation to a student. See Robert T. Kennedy, "McGrath, Maida, Michiels: Introduction to a Study of the Canonical and Civil Law Status of Church Related Institutions in the United States," *The Jurist* 50, no. 2 (1990): 351–401. McGrath left The Catholic University of America to become acting president at Saint Mary's College, Notre Dame in 1967 and was elected president in 1968. He died suddenly in June 1970.

2. *Horace Mann League v Board of Public Works of Maryland.* See chapter 1, note 30 for full citation.

3. The process of getting a state charter varied from state to state and even to pre-state federal territories. The naming of lay trustees in some cases was a response to the anti-Catholic spirit present in some places and at certain historical periods. In other instances, securing a separate civil charter had simply not been seen as necessary.

4. According to a letter from the then president, Robert A. Kidera, to a Dr. W. H. Cowley in September 1975, the board was "an autonomous self-perpetuating board of trustees." By the time of this letter, the board had three clergymen and eighteen laymen. Kidera does not say what was the role of the bishop; ACUA-NCEA. In a letter issued by the local Ordinary, Bishop Walter Curtis, on the first anniversary of the founding of Sacred Heart, April 15, 1964, he wrote that Pope Paul VI had expressed his pleasure that "under the wise supervision of the diocesan authority, this institution of higher learning will be directed and staffed by laity." ACNR, Mary Robert Falls, O.S.U., Presidential Papers 1963–1970.

5. In terms of the "network" active in the matter of independent boards, the gathering at Loretto Heights was a significant step. A conference report was issued in December 1968, edited by Francis J. Kerins, a faculty member at Loretto Heights and later president of Carroll College. He, John McGrath, Paul Reinert, S.J., Gerald Dupont, S.S.E., Earl McGrath, Jacqueline Grennan, S.L., John Walsh, C.S.C., and Raymond Fleck, C.S.C., were among the seminar leaders; McGrath's work was required reading, and approximately 130 college and university presidents, trustees, and experts in higher education attended. This report is an excellent source for the mentality regarding the new movement toward governance by independent boards which predominated in 1967–68 among the leaders in Catholic higher education.

6. Friedman, in a letter to members on May 12, 1967, urged them to cooperate with McGrath by sending their bylaws to him for his study. In a second letter, on January 2, 1968, Friedman reported to the members that he had been successful in helping McGrath in obtaining funds from the Raskob Foundation; ACUA-NCEA.

7. For background on Horgan, see the section on College of New Rochelle in chapter 2. The opinion referred to here is from his paper prepared for the trustees of the College of New Rochelle; ACNR, Board of Trustees, 1966.

8. James O'Connor, S.J., "Some Phases of Administrative Authority from a Canonical Viewpoint," in JEA *Proceedings* of Committee on Colleges and Universities, 1966–67, Appendix D. This paper was also used to stimulate discussion at the May 1967 "Orientation Workshop" described in the section on Saint Louis University in chapter 2.

9. This proposal is not really a solution because, according to Robert Kennedy, such an arrangement would not protect the canonical requirement that decisions in certain financial matters had to be made by the "provincial with the consent of the council." Letter to the author from Rev. Robert Kennedy, March 20, 1995.

10. J. McGrath, *Catholic Institutions: Canonical and Civil Law Status*, p. 24

11. Ibid., p. 34. McGrath did point out, however, that it was better not to have religious officials serve *ex officio* on boards since other "better informed" trustees could be found within the religious community (p. 35).

12. According to Robert Kennedy, this contention of McGrath, while true according to civil law, was false in the case of many (probably most) Catholic colleges and universities according to canon law. Letter from Kennedy to the author, March 20, 1995.

13. Robert Henle, S.J., had made the same point in a memorandum to Father Reinert, in response to his request for feedback on his proposal in 1966; ASLU.

14. Very little has been written about diocesan colleges and their governance structures. Rev. John F. Murphy is currently collecting data from them so that an analysis can be done in the near future. Preliminary summary of information received by Father Murphy was shared with the author in February 1996.

15. It was reviewed by John R. Schmidt of The Catholic University of America in *The Jurist* 28 (1968): 228–35. The review,

however, was simply a summary of the main thesis and gave little attention to critique.

16. J. C. Ford, S.J., "Remarks as Chairman of first session of Round Hill meeting," May 26, 1967. Unpublished paper, AMPSJ.

17. Ruth Cessna, Jur.D., "John J. McGrath: The Mask of Divestiture and Disaffiliation," unpublished paper, San Francisco, 1971, ACUA-NCEA. In a letter transmitting Cessna's work to Rev. A. William Crandell, S.J., at AJCU, Rev. John H. Martin, S.J., of the University of San Francisco wrote that Father Andrew C. Varga, S.J., "speaking for Father General," authorized him to have Miss Cessna compose this thesis for submission to the twenty-eight presidents and the rectors of the separately incorporated communities on college campuses. "Father General wishes the presidents and rectors to submit the thesis to legal counsel for an evaluation." Letter of May 12, 1971, AAJCU.

18. Dexter Hanley, S.J., memorandum to Board of Governors, AJCU, January 8, 1972; AAJCU. Handwritten at the end of the document are various dates: approval by the board of directors, 1-8-72; forwarded to Jesuit provincials and Father General Arrupe, 2-1-72; approval given to position paper by Father Arrupe at Rome meeting, 2-5-72. I have found no response from AJCU to Miss Cessna nor any further reference by other canonists.

19. Confidential memo from Gibbons to Fitterer, AAJCU. In the AJCU files it is attached to the Dexter Hanley memorandum. Gibbons was concerned about the "positivistic" outlook toward ecclesiastical law that he found among some American canonists and the Canon Law Society of America. He suggested that this trend should be taken into account when reviewing McGrath's work. He also pointed out that he had not received the Cessna paper so there was some difficulty in responding to Hanley's critique. I have been unable to identify William Gibbons.

20. By the early 1970s some questions were being raised about the nearly universal acceptance of McGrath's position. In an article entitled "Canon Law/Civil Law Status of Catholic Hospitals," in *Hospital Progress* of September 4, 1973, Rev. Adam Maida, a canon and a civil lawyer, commented: "The unchal-

lenged receptivity of this theory and its conclusions throughout the country is utterly amazing." Maida said that McGrath "has done what Henry VIII, Napoleon, and Lenin have done," i.e., secularized church property.

21. Stamm, "Emerging Models of Governance." See chapter 1, note 12.

22. Francis X. Gallagher, "Observations arising from the *Horace Mann* Case," NCEA Bulletin, *Proceedings* 63 (1966). Note that his talk was given to the Committee on Federal Relations at the NCEA Convention April 11–14. The decision in the case was announced on June 2.

23. Communication from Robert D. Stone, Counsel and Deputy Commissioner for Legal Affairs, The University of the State of New York, June 13, 1968, distributed to presidents of private colleges and universities in New York under date of August 5, 1968, with a note explaining that the criteria come from *Horace Mann* and are considered relevant to the New York State constitutional situation; ACNR, Mary Robert Falls, O.S.U., Presidential Papers 1963–1970. See also the discussion about the Bundy money in the section on Fordham in chapter 2.

24. See also Edward Michael O'Keefe, "The Influence of New York State aid to Private colleges and universities on the process of change taking place in Catholic institutions" (Ph.D. dissertation, SUNY Buffalo, 1974). There are several dissertations that have tried to measure the impact of Bundy money on New York State Catholic colleges and universities, but since many of the same changes occurred in other states as well as in New York, it is hard to know exactly what to attribute to Bundy and what to other social and religious changes of the 1960s and 1970s.

25. William Stauder, S.J., to Daniel C. O'Connell, S.J., August 27, 1974, ASLU.

26. Stamm, "Emerging Models of Governance," and "Report on the Governance of American Catholic Higher Education Institutions," *Current Issues in Catholic Higher Education* 14, no. 1 (Summer 1993): 10–15. In the second survey, Stamm received 125

completed questionnaires from the 228 to whom he had sent them.

27. Mr. Wilson has given his reflections in a brochure entitled *Tilton v. Richardson: The Search for Sectarianism in Education*, printed by the Association of American Colleges, Washinton, D.C., 1971. The defendant colleges were Fairfield University, Sacred Heart University, Albertus Magnus College, and Annhurst College. Wilson has also prepared a later reflection which was in draft form in March 1994 but has not yet been published. A copy of the draft is in the possession of the author of this work. Reference for *Tilton v Richardson* is 403 US 672 (1971).

28. In the process of defending the colleges, NCEA promoted a campaign to assist them with funds and amicus briefs. A special effort was made to solicit funds from bishops, and the executive director of the College and University Department reported some success—about $95,000. Letter of Rev. Clarence Friedman to Most Rev. Stanislaus J. Brzana, D.D., Bishop of Ogdensburg, New York, May 12, 1971, ACUA-NCEA.

29. In this connection see the affirmation of the 1976 NCEA study, "Relations of American Catholic Colleges and Universities with the Church," and the 1980 *Catholic Higher Education and the Pastoral Mission of the Church,* which is a statement of the NCCB. Reprinted in Gallin, *American Catholic Higher Education,* pp. 71–86 and 135–51, respectively.

30. Edmund Ryan to board of trustees, July 1968; AFU, PM63.

31. This point is made in a memorandum prepared by Sister Hildegarde Marie Mahoney, S.C., for the Fiscal Concerns Committee of the Leadership Conference of Women Religious on February 2, 1974. She urged the committee not to adopt unquestioningly the opinion of McGrath nor to think that Maida's treatment of the issues was definitive. She emphasized the complexity of the questions and commented on the lack of competent canonical advice even in larger institutions that have their own legal counsel for civil matters on a regular retainer fee. On the other hand, "If they [administrators] consult Canon Law, they

find that requirements relative to borrowing, for example, are so antiquated and inapplicable to the operation of a modern college or hospital that they seek some relief. Maybe they resort to epikeia if they are aware of it." ANCCB, Committee on Law and Public Policy file on McGrath/Maida.

32. Kennedy, "McGrath, Maida, Michiels," pp. 363–4, refers to this letter, and calls attention to the fact that although a private letter, it was published in *Canon Law Digest* 9 (1982): 367–69.

33. Tabera and Garrone to Krol, October 7, 1974; ANCCB, Committee on Law and Public Policy file, PROT.N. SCRIS 300/74; SCI 427/70/23.

34. Resolution of the Committee on Law and Public Policy, Report of committee meeting, December 14, 1974; ANCCB, under date of January 3, 1975.

35. Minutes of the Meeting of the Joint Commission on Ownership of Catholic Institutions, January 24, 1975, ANCCB. Members of the commission present at that meeting were Archbishop Daniel Sheehan, Bishop Joseph Daley, Bishop John May, Rev. Paul Boyle, C.P., Rev. William Lewers, C.S.C., Sr. Assunta Stang, S.C., and Sr. Hildegarde Mahoney, S.C.

36. Adam J. Maida, *Ownership, Control and Sponsorship of Catholic Institutions: A Practical Guide* (Harrisburg, Pa.: Pennsylvania Catholic Conference, 1975). Bernardin seems to have been following the advice of the legal counsel at USCC as to the use of Maida for guidelines. This work of Maida was distributed to all the bishops by the Pennsylvania Catholic Conference.

37. Archbishop Joseph Bernardin to Auturo Cardinal Tabera and Gabriel Cardinal Garrone, March 6, 1975; ANCCB PROT.N. SCI 427/70/23; SCRIS 300/74.

38. Garrone to the presidents of Episcopal Conferences, April 10, 1974, ANCCB. He instructed them to set up a committee within the episcopal conference "which is expressly given the job of handling Catholic University problems." The Congregation saw these problems as involving the "tensions between the magisterium of the Church and the demands of academic free-

dom." One can see in this letter the beginning of the long dialogue between Rome and Catholic universities worldwide which led to *Ex Corde Ecclesiae,* issued in 1990. For the 1972 document "The Catholic University in the Modern World," and related letter of Garrone, see Gallin, *American Catholic Higher Education,* pp. 37–61.

39. John F. Murphy to Frederick R. McManus, May 20, 1975;. McManus file, ACUA-NCEA

40. Philip R. Moots and Edward McGlynn Gaffney Jr., *Church and Campus* (Notre Dame, Ind.: University of Notre Dame Press, 1979); and Edward McGlynn Gaffney Jr. and Philip Moots, *Government and Campus* (Notre Dame, Ind.: University of Notre Dame Press, 1982). Of particular help is Appendix A in the latter volume, entitled "The Present State of Roman Catholic Canon Law regarding Colleges and Sponsoring Religious Bodies." This was prepared by Rev. James E. Coriden and Rev. Frederick R. McManus. It is important to place it in the context of the 1977 draft of the revised canon law which had just been received for comment. This appendix also contains a brief but significant critique of both McGrath and Maida.

41. See Kennedy, "McGrath, Maida, Michiels," cited in note 1. As we have seen, the basis for the debate from a scholarly canonical perspective was, for the most part, the work of two men who were both civil and canon lawyers: John McGrath and Adam Maida. Today, both of their theories are understood to have weaknesses which were not perceived by their followers at the time.

Conclusion

1. Garrone and Tabera to Krol, October 7, 1974, cited in chapter 3.

2. Gallin, *American Catholic Higher Education,* Parts II, III, and IV. The dialogue continues in the work of the bishops' committee set up in 1991 to apply the norms of *ECE* to the American context.

3. This summary is located in the ACCU Administration files for 1970–1980 and unfortunately has no author or date. It is simply titled "A Summary of some responses to Cardinal Garrone's letter to American Catholic Colleges of Oct. 7, 1974"; ACCU Office Files.

Index

About the Author

Alice Gallin, O.S.U., is Visiting Research Scholar at The Catholic University of America. For the academic year 1996–97 she is Visiting Professor at Saint Louis University. Her study of German universities, *Midwives of Nazism,* was published by Mercer University in 1986. Her most recent publication is *American Catholic Higher Education: Essential Documents* (Notre Dame Press, 1992).